Innovating Talent Attraction

INNOVATING TALENT ATTRACTION

A Practitioner's Guide for Cities, Regions and Countries

Marcus Andersson, Morten King-Grubert and Nikolaj Lubanski

GettyImages:
– p. 8/9: Spain, Bizkaia province, Bilbao (Juan Carlos Muoz)
– p. 24/25: Berlin (RICOWde)
– p. 40/41: Singapore (JeremyHui)
– p. 58/59: Toronto (d3sign)
– p. 72/73: Austin (Victoria Chen)
– p. 92/93: Tel Aviv (Ilan Shacham)
– p. 112/113: Eindhoven (Allan Baxter)
– p. 126/127: Santiago (SWL Fotografia)
– p. 144/145: Tampere (Stuart Forster/robertharding)

Innovating Talent Attraction
A Practitioner's Guide for Cities, Regions and Countries
Marcus Andersson, Morten King-Grubert and Nikolaj Lubanski
© The authors and U Press 2016
Cover: Ordered by Colour
Type: Cambria and ScalaSans
Paper: Arctic Volume White 130 g
Graphic design, prepress and printing: Narayana Press
Printed in Denmark 2016
ISBN 978-87-93060-37-1

U Press
Rådhuspladsen 16
DK-1550 Copenhagen
www.upress.dk

Contents

1 **Introduction** 11
    Why a book on innovating talent attraction? 12
    How big a problem is talent scarcity? 14
    Your guide – from one practitioner to another 17

Interview with Merlind Hinz, SKF Group 21

2 **Talent Attraction Management – what is it and why does it need to be managed?** 27
    What factors influence talented people's choice of place? 27
    So is it the job or the lifestyle that make talents relocate? 29
    How can places attract and retain talent? 29
    What is Talent Attraction Management? 30
    It is a team effort 33
    What skills do you need to manage and orchestrate this complex multi-stakeholder setting? 34

Interview with Charlotte Mark, Microsoft 37

3 **Talent Attraction Management in practice – The Copenhagen Case** 43
    The Copenhagen case: From FDI to talent attraction 44
    Adding the missing link – a regional talent strategy 47
    The product portfolio: Concrete tools catering to international talent 49
    From Copenhagen to the rest of the world 53

Interview with Paul Evans, INSEAD 55

4 **Strategic Recommendations for Successful Talent Attraction Management** 61
    Engaging talents as ambassadors 62
    Engage employers 64

    Interregional talent sharing: From foes to friends   67
    Find your niche: Competitive advantage and authenticity   68
    Disrupt and innovate to differentiate   69

5 How to organise for Talent Attraction Management   75

    Organisational structure to optimise talent attraction and retention   75
    Governance and funding models   82
    Creating public–private partnerships – how public institutions and private business can work together   83
    From theory to practice – how change management can help you get started   84

Interview with Yvonne van Hest, Brainport Development   89

6 Talent Attraction and Place Branding   95

    Six branding objectives   95
    Four principles of innovative place branding   98
    Marketing strategies and campaigns in practice   100

Interview with HRH Prince Joachim, Danish Monarchy   109

7 Attracting Entrepreneurial Talent   115

    Entrepreneurial reality   115
    Tools and recommendations for entrepreneurial talent attraction   117
    Promote a positive image of entrepreneurship   118
    Start-up communities and co-working spaces   119
    Entrepreneurship education and the long-term approach   120
    Differentiate and find your talent niche   121
    Leverage the international community   122

Interview with Manas Mani, Nordea   123

8 On the future of talent attraction – is more innovation needed?   129

    Will talent attraction still be high on the agenda in the coming years?   130

From the 'war for talent' to talent mobility collaboration　133
　　　Merging the agendas of domestic and international talent　135
　　　Cities and regions are the new locus for talent attraction　136
　　　Are we ready for true brain circulation?　138
　　　The new black: Management style and lifestyle as attraction factors　139
　　　Is innovation in talent attraction still needed?　140

About the authors　147

Acknowledgements　149

Appendix overview　151

Appendix 1 – Regional assessment survey　153
　　　Regional Assessment Survey　155

Appendix 2 – Cases　156
　　　Case 1:　Austin mini case – Attracting talent by supporting creativity　156
　　　Case 2:　Berlin mini case – The role of the public sector in an organically developed ecosystem　157
　　　Case 3:　Bizkaia mini case – A network-model approach to talent attraction　159
　　　Case 4:　Chile mini case – Building a brand by going against the grain　160
　　　Case 5:　Brainport mini case – From the war for talent to talent sharing　162
　　　Case 6:　Singapore mini case – A key pillar in the country's economic strategy　163
　　　Case 7:　Tampere mini case – Providing local help to talents　164
　　　Case 8:　Tel Aviv mini case – Entrepreneurial culture　166
　　　Case 9:　Toronto mini case – Immigration policy as a talent magnet　167

1 Introduction

The meeting room is full, as the topic on the agenda has become one of the most important factors for creating regional economic growth in recent years.

All the right people for the occasion are present. Government agencies, the mayor's office, the regional economic development board, deans of universities, and CEOs of local companies with their HR and employer branding teams, to name a few.

The stage is set and the participants are fully aware that a lot is at stake. This question must be answered.

Nikolaj Lubanski, Director of Talent at Copenhagen Capacity and co-author of this book, starts his presentation with the following information:

1. There is a mismatch between what is being taught at Danish universities and the skills required by businesses. Soon, Denmark will lack thousands of engineers and science graduates. You can add the demographical challenge to this problem; Denmark has a skewed workforce, with a large proportion of workers close to retirement age and smaller numbers from younger generations coming into the workforce. In summary, there is a skills and demographical mismatch between supply and demand.

2. Greater Copenhagen is not a known career destination. Despite Denmark and Copenhagen often being ranked in global top 10s for everything from 'ease of doing business' to 'happiest people in the world', the region is often not on the radar of the world's bright minds. Furthermore, few Danish companies are well-known enough, or big enough, to attract the best candidates from abroad.

3. The international competition for talent is massive. More and more cities, regions and countries around the world are investing heavily in this aspect of recruitment.

These facts are the prerequisite for this book. They tell the story of why Greater Copenhagen needs to attract and retain international talent. However, neither the meeting nor the problem is unique to Copenhagen and Denmark. In fact, access to skilled competences is increasingly becoming a key challenge for economic development and growth in most regions around the world.

Over the past few years, the authors have discussed this challenge with entities in the field of talent attraction and retention from Copenhagen to Chile. Berlin to Bizkaia. Stockholm to Scotland. Tel Aviv to Toronto – and many places in between.

We know meetings just like the one outlined above are taking place in hundreds of other locations worldwide. How does a city, region or country stand out as an attractive talent destination? In a world where the competition for the attention of bright minds is becoming more and more fierce, you need to do something extraordinary. It does not make sense to do the same as everyone else. This calls for an innovative approach to talent attraction.

In April and May of 2016, we gathered together practitioners whose talent attraction efforts were made on behalf of cities, regions and nations from 10 different countries to discuss best practices and principles in the industry. Following the second of two very inspiring discussions and knowledge-sharing events over the course of four days, one attendee said.

"It would really be helpful to my daily work to have an executive summary of all these topics we have covered together."

That executive summary turned into this book.

Why a book on innovating talent attraction?

This book is intended as a practitioner's guide for those people acting on behalf of cities, regions and countries to attract and retain international competences; it seeks to identify both their strategies and rationales. Simply put, it tells the story of the key regional challenge of places like Greater Copenhagen, of which there are many, around the world.

What can we do about the problem?

It is a problem that has more consequences on regional growth than one might at first consider. Access to talent is, in our experience, increasingly becoming one of the most important decision-making factors for international investors when establishing a new regional headquarters, sales office or R&D facility, and the like. And let us be honest: most regions are very competitively trying to lure these investments in to bring more jobs and growth. On the flipside, already existing companies located in the region are also increasingly finding access to talent to be one of their key drivers of growth. Without it, they may need to move their activities abroad or outsource large components of it. Again, the result is bad business – or no business to be precise – for the region and its inhabitants.

Our aim in this book is to support the process of renewing the approach to international talent attraction and retention. By gathering the newest knowledge and best-case examples from different locations in Europe and the world, the book will work as a guide for countries, regions and cities who would like to be market leaders in the competition for the worlds' best brains.

We recognise that the topic of talent attraction is not a new one. The ground-breaking McKinsey study of the late 1990s exposed the "war for talent" as a strategic business challenge and a critical driver of corporate performance.[1] Following the dot-com bubble and recent financial crisis, it would have been easy to make the fatal assumption that the war for talent is over. In fact, it is only just beginning. The competitive landscape has now spread across cities, regions and countries – and the competition for talent is poised to become one of the defining economic issues of the 21st century. It is even tempting to go so far as to state that today human capital is replacing financial capital as the engine of economic prosperity – or at least we are moving in that direction.

In this context, allow us to highlight a paradox of significant proportions. Despite a growing global population, the availability of skilled talent is actually shrinking. In Europe, 2010 marked a turning point, as it was the first year in which the number of labour market entrants fell lower than that of

---

1 Michaels, Handfield-Jones, & Axelrod (2001)

retiring workers.[2] In about two-thirds of OECD countries, the proportion of the total population that was of working age declined in 2011.[3] The emerging markets, such as China and Russia for example, are in a similar situation. The demographic forecasts are critical. Employers across the globe face the challenge, despite a growing global population, of recruiting from a shrinking workforce, leading to intensified competition for talents.

Add to that another paradox: In many countries the unemployment rate is still relatively high in spite of a growing economy, but the unemployment queue predominantly contains workers with no or limited competences related to the market demand. They are not the skilled workforce that is needed.

We are in other words entering a new era with an unprecedented scarcity of talented people, a problem which if left unaddressed will severely impede economic growth locally and internationally, regardless of where in the world you call home.

In the not too distant future, the world will need millions of new business professionals, engineers, IT specialists, scientific researchers, technicians, and many more workers in knowledge-intensive roles. In the not too distant future, these people may not be available.

How big a problem is talent scarcity?

Let us make the talent and skill scarcity apparent by looking at some numbers.

A global survey from Manpower Group showed that 38 percent of nearly 41,000 employers surveyed globally in 2015 reported difficulties in finding staff with the right skills – the highest shortage since the start of the recession in 2007.[4]

To simply sustain economic growth, by 2030 the United States will need to add more than 25 million workers to its workforce, and Western Europe will need to add more than 45 million.[5]

2   Ernst & Young (2010)
3   OECD (2015)
4   ManpowerGroup (2015)
5   World Economic Forum (2011)

Compared to today, in 2050, most of the G7 – representing almost two-thirds of net global wealth[6] – and BRIC countries will have more than doubled age 65+ dependency ratios, and all except India will have more aged societies than today's most aged society (Japan)[7].

The number of individuals aged 60+ is growing rapidly in China, already forming 12.5 percent of the nation's population. Taking the country's one-child policy and its drop in birth rates into account, by 2050 the 10 workers currently supporting each senior citizen will fall to 2.5 workers. Employability will continue to be a huge problem worldwide. Because of the uneven quality of education systems, estimates suggest that only 25 percent of Indian and 20 percent of Russian professionals are currently considered employable by multinationals.[8]

As a result, attracting talents from one's own country and even neighbouring countries might increasingly risk becoming a zero-sum game – stepping up competition even further. This war for talent will become increasingly acute in sectors that require high skill levels and more education, but if we as regions promote better international mobility, we can mend this trend.

But what about supply? Globalisation in itself is fuelling mobility and it is fair to say that we live in an 'age of mobility'. The world is getting smaller and on a personal and professional level, we are interconnected like never before. More and more companies are international from the get-go, if not already born global. Meanwhile, employees shift between headquarters in one country to subsidiaries in other countries, through expat assignments as well as simply pursuing international opportunities in general.

There are some interesting facts about this state of affairs that are relevant to the problem of a shrinking workforce.[9]

The Millennial generation – defined as people born between 1982 and 1999 – is now entering the labour force in larger numbers and research shows that many of them wish to gain international work experience.

---

6   Crédit Suisse (2013)
7   World Economic Forum (2011)
8   World Economic Forum (2011)
9   World Economic Forum (2011)

There are an estimated 214 million international migrants worldwide. Collectively, they could make up the world's fifth-largest nation.

In North and West Africa more than one quarter of the population is under the age of 15 and unemployment rates for young people exceed 30 percent.

Migration is not only a south to north phenomenon; 40 percent of the world's migrants move from one developing country to another.

It is fair to say, then, that talent is moving across borders. Looking at Europe specifically, we argue that the internal mobility between countries could be much higher.

Likewise, the skills gap is also connected to a mismatch between the competences needed in companies and the patterns in the output from the educational system. Too many pursue an education that is not required by the labour market.

Some countries and regions are more fortunate than others and have a natural inflow of international talents – the reason being that either the brand, lifestyle or cluster competence is so strong that by default this is the place to be. To use two simple examples from the US: think Hollywood if you are an actor, or Silicon Valley if you are an IT entrepreneur.

Most regions are not that fortunate. Even though your region may be in various top 10 rankings ranging from ease of doing business, liveability, happiness index and income level, to the quality of academic institutions, and as such have a brand appeal by default, this alone does not secure a steady natural inflow of international talents. If nobody knows you exist or where you are located, it does not matter. No, Copenhagen is not the capital of Sweden and Danes do not speak Dutch, to name a few – believe it or not – quite normal examples from Danes in conversation with non-Danes around the world. Similar cases can be made for many countries – even in this day and age of our knowledge-based societies.

But whose problem is this? From our perspective you cannot blame your target group for misplacing the Nordic capitals; the finger points back at you. In short, disregard how 'cool' you believe your region is perceived to be internationally. Branding is necessary, and your story needs to travel beyond your borders. Let us be honest though – this is not a book about branding. We have met with branding experts from all over the world. And they are that: experts. If you want to excel in this area, you need them. Our advice is to read this book first and then call them, when you are ready to attract international talent. Meanwhile, we will of course include as much insight as we have gained from them. But our concept is to lay the groundwork first. In doing so, we do not seek to produce an academic publication. You need the academics to get your data right. However, we want to give you a practitioner's version of how to develop a city, region or nation's efforts towards increasing the inflow of international competences to the place you call home.

Your guide – from one practitioner to another

What you have in your hands offers the experience and knowledge of one practitioner to another. Well, to be exact, it is a guide composed by the three of us, and ultimately it also originates from thousands of enlightening discussions around the world with governments, regions, cities, universities, companies, the aforementioned branding experts and academics, and international mobile workforces themselves. We will share cases from some of the leading cities and regions performing at the top of their class, as well as interviews with relevant stakeholders, to illustrate different perspectives on the issues pertaining to the industry.

As we outline the premises for this book, we recognise that in our experience the focal point for talent attraction and retention is moving from the national to the regional and city level. The need for combining talent attraction with place branding adds to this tendency: cities are becoming more well-known than countries. The current trends all point to a severe need for innovating talent attraction and retention. As more and more entities are entering the same game, you need to stand out. The million-dollar question is, of course, how do you do that?

As a starting point, we would like to emphasise the three main components of successful Talent Attraction Management that permeate this book:

- Innovation: Being innovative and experimental – even disruptive
- Inclusiveness: Working with your stakeholders and target groups
- Embracing mobility: More mobility leads to diversity; diversity leads to innovation. Mobility is set to increase in the future and take new forms – and working with Talent Attraction Management can help promote mobility and therefore innovation.

If you lack innovation in the way you work with talent attraction and the solutions you come up with, you will fail to stand out. If you just replicate what others do or try to pretend that you are a city like New York when you are not, you will most likely not see an increase in the number of internationals coming your way. Actually, not being New York is the reason why inclusiveness is needed. You need to work intensively together with your local stakeholders and target groups in order to identify the assets of your location. If you oversell your destination, those you attract will be disappointed, as their experience will be different from what you promised. And they will share their bad experience in their international networks, which may well make up your target group. This is also why you need to embrace mobility. Even if some of the internationals you attract only stay for three years or fewer before moving on to pursue a career somewhere else, make sure they leave as ambassadors for your destination. This will lead to a further influx of skilled people. What is more, there is growing evidence that more diverse places, organisations and teams foster creativity and innovation, which are of the utmost importance to today's economy.

This is not a book you need to read from beginning to end. You may do so of course. However, we also encourage you to check out the different topics outlined below and then start with what is most relevant to you. As international talents are becoming more and more mobile and literally fly all over the world to fulfil their career ambitions, we also recognise that the cities and regions working to attracting them are in different stages of preparation to attract, welcome and retain international competences. Using the analogy of flying, some may be parked at the gate, while others are ready to board, still others may be delayed or in transfer, while some are safely in flight towards their final destination.

In this chapter, we set the scene, introducing the importance of talent attraction and retention for cities, regions and countries. In Chapter Two, we introduce a model for working with talent attraction and retention. We call it the Talent Attraction Management (TAM) model.

Chapter Three shows how the TAM model can be implemented by sharing the story of Copenhagen, where a comprehensive talent attraction and retention strategy with multiple innovative activities has been implemented.

In Chapter Four, we turn to concrete *s*trategic recommendations for successful Talent Attraction Management. We will look in depth at certain regions/cities that are on the cutting edge of talent attraction and retention, and share key learning points, seeking to investigate what the best do and what we can learn from them.

There are several ways to approach the optimisation of talent attraction and retention. In Chapter Five, we introduce different governance models, touching on some best practices of how public institutions and private business work together, while providing advice on starting up the process.

Whereas the earlier chapters deal with the more strategic and organisational level of talent attraction and retention, Chapter Six will dive into the practicalities of how you actually can attract talent by understanding what makes a place attractive for internationals and what the best practices are, from the perspectives of cities, regions and nations.

Entrepreneurs are also mobile and internationally minded, which brings us to Chapter Seven. Here we pinpoint what cities and regions can do to attract founders and start-ups, as well as helping them grow.

Finally, in Chapter Eight, we try to look to the future of Talent Attraction Management. What do we expect to happen within the field of talent attraction and retention? Will the current tendencies continue or will the agenda change?

As the book is a practitioner's guide, we hope it will inspire you to either start your journey in this field or optimise your current efforts. For both cases, we offer a self-assessment survey in Appendix 1, helping you to identify where to prioritise your resources. Likewise, in Appendix 2, there are nine cases of regions and cities from around the world that stand out as best practice examples within talent attraction and retention.

In between the chapters, we present interviews with key stakeholders and knowledge leaders relevant to most regions, who offer their own perspectives on the issues we cover in the book.

References

Ernst and Young (2010). *Managing Today's Global Workforce: Evaluating Talent Management to Improve Business.* London: Ernst and Young.

ManpowerGroup (2015). *Talent shortage survey.* http://www.manpowergroup.com/wps/wcm/connect/db23c560-08b6-485f-9bf6-f5f38a43c76a/2015_Talent_Shortage_Survey_US-lo_res.pdf?MOD=AJPERES. Accessed September 30, 2016.

Michaels, E., Handfield-Jones, H., & Axelrod, B. (2001). *The War for Talent.* Harvard Business Press.

Niedomysl, T. & Hansen, H.K. (2010). What matters more for the decision to move: jobs versus amenities. *Environment and Planning A* 42(7).

OECD (2015). *International Migration Outlook 2015.* OECD Publishing. DOI: http://dx.doi.org/10.1787/migr_outlook-2015-en. Accessed September 30, 2016.

Crédit Suisse (2013). Global wealth report 2013. *Zurich: Crédit Suisse* https://publications.credit-suisse.com/tasks/render/file/?fileID=BCDB1364-A105-0560-1332EC9100FF5C83. Accessed September 30, 2016.

World Economic Forum (2011). *Global Talent Risk – Seven Responses.* http://www3.weforum.org/docs/PS_WEF_GlobalTalentRisk_Report_2011.pdf. Accessed September 30, 2016.

Interview with Merlind Hinz, SKF Group

Head of market communications, Vehicle Aftermarket at SKF Group in Gothenburg, Sweden

Photo: Barry Li/Business Region Göteborg

Merlind, you are from Berlin, one of the hottest talent magnets in Europe – how did you end up in Gothenburg?

I moved to Gothenburg because of love. I have lived here for three and a half years now and really enjoy it.

How did the transition to Gothenburg work?

It worked quite well all in all. I had some difficulties finding housing; it is a different housing market system compared to what I am used to, and that is sometimes hard to understand and manage when you are foreigner. Socially I found good networks to connect to other foreigners, but it has been more difficult to connect to local people. The whole getting the daily life to work is always a big struggle when you are new in a place; everything from how to book a doctor's appointment to understanding how the social security system works is a challenge – especially if you can only find the information you need in the local language and not English. Luckily many people at the relevant government authorities speak English and were helpful.

How can a region help in such an endeavour?

To listen to us – those that have made the move to the region – is a good start, which this area is doing. I also think a buddy system would be very good to have in place, to get assigned a contact person you can talk to when you are new in a place. I also think it is important for regions to look at best practices from other regions internationally and learn how to improve.

How did you find a job? How can the region help in this process?

It was very easy for me to find work but I have acquaintances and people I know from networks that struggled hard to find one, especially those who did not speak Swedish.

I soon realised that coffee breaks play an important role in workplaces in Sweden, and knowing Swedish is very much an advantage in fitting in socially. One way the region can help is to make it easier to learn Swedish, by making sure that there are language courses that meet the needs of international talent.

How important is the place itself, in comparison to the specific university or employer, when you choose to move?

I think you move mainly to a job, but if the place does not live up to expectations, you maybe only stay for one or two years for the job, and then move on to another place. So, in order for regions to retain talent, they need to ensure that people can have a good life outside their jobs.

How should a region promote itself to be attractive for international talent?

You first need to ask yourself: attractive for whom? For example, when I came three and a half years ago I was not interested in knowing about childcare benefits or how the school system worked, but rather I wanted a fun life with culture, shopping and good travel connections. But more mature expats of course want more focus on schools and childcare. You need to realise that you cannot be one thing for all international talents, as a region.

What are the benefits of moving to a new place? What has it given you as an individual?

It has broadened my horizon. I am definitely a different person after this experience, and it is a great way to develop your cultural sensitivity by looking outside the culture you grew up with. For personal development it's amazing how much you mature from the experience and I would say it has enriched my life immensely.

And of course it is super exciting, every day! To give you an example: in the first year, even trips to the supermarket are an adventure.

Taking this step is something that I would not have missed for anything; it has been so valuable to me.

Interview with Merlind Hinz, SKF Group

2 Talent Attraction Management – what is it and why does it need to be managed?

In this chapter we will discuss why people relocate to other places, and what factors influence the choice of a given place. We will also go deeper into the concept of Talent Attraction Management – what it is and how it can be managed and coordinated.

What factors influence talented people's choice of place?

The debate on place vs jobs has probably not escaped anyone that takes an interest in talent attraction, mobility of people and economic development of places – that is, do people first and foremost move to a new place because of a new job opportunity or because of the qualities of the place?

Richard Florida – one of the biggest proponents of the idea that people choose places because of their qualities, lifestyle opportunities and vibe – would say: place comes first! Others, like many economic geographers who study place attractiveness,[10] would claim that people choose jobs first, and then places.

In our experience, this is not a simple either/or question. It really depends on multiple factors. But before we go deeper into this issue, let us first take a look at what makes people leave a place to pursue opportunities elsewhere – and why do they choose to go to a certain place?

There are a number of factors that help explain this. The reason why someone leaves a location is a *push factor*, and the reason why someone moves to a particular new location is a *pull factor*. When it comes to labour mobility, one of the strongest push effects comes from a lack of economic opportunity. When an area offers too few jobs and professional opportunities, some of its residents will feel compelled to leave in pursuit of careers elsewhere.

Cultural and lifestyle factors also come into consideration: if a place is seen as undynamic and 'boring', especially by young(er) professionals, they may move to places that offer a more vibrant cultural and social life.

---

10   Niedomysl & Hansen (2010)

If a society or region as a whole is perceived as embodying an intolerant and closed social atmosphere, it may contribute to pushing people away, especially those belonging to minority groups. Furthermore, it will also limit the likelihood of an international workforce relocating to this region.

Finally – albeit it is difficult to do anything about – weather can play a role as a push factor, and especially harsh and dark winters can have a negative effect on location decisions.[11]

Just like push factors, those that pull talents to regions can involve both employment and lifestyle considerations.

We believe that those attracted by international employment opportunities fall into two categories. Firstly, many talents with specialised skills and knowledge seek career advancement, and are keen to work in businesses that are on the cutting edge of their industry. These people will be drawn to larger regions and regions that have particular strongholds of excellence within the professional area of the talent in question. The market leaders, most innovative companies and fast growing companies in the industry will either be already located in this region or in the process of setting up an entity.

We can call this the 'cluster argument', as the presence of a cluster indicates that there will be other opportunities for people who move to the region, besides just the initial job offer at the firm. A person who moves for one job knows there will be other opportunities to find career advancing positions in other firms. This is especially important in sectors where fixed-term jobs are common.[12]

The second employment pull factor comes from the higher levels of productivity in a given region, often indicated by the fact that earnings are higher in that particular region. Many young Swedes go to Norway to work because earnings are higher in Norway. This factor also helps explain the migration from developing economies to advanced economies. We can call this the 'earnings argument'.

In addition, lifestyle factors and language play a role as pull factors. Most people have noticed that Berlin has become one of the hottest entrepre-

---

11 International Regions Benchmarking Consortium (2009)
12 For example, studies of the Hollywood film cluster have indicated that skilled workers in the film industry choose to remain close to this large pool of employment opportunities to offset risks associated with short-term contractual work common in film production (Christopherson & Storper, 1987).

neurial and creative talent magnets in Europe, largely thanks to a vibrant cultural, nightlife and music scene, combined with low accommodation and office costs. And compared to a decade ago, you can now manage your life using English as the main language. You need a common language to communicate and conduct business. This is why English-speaking countries automatically have an advantage when it comes to talent attraction – an advantage that is becoming less prominent as the populations of many other countries continuously improve their English skills.

So is it the job or the lifestyle that make talents relocate?

In our experience, which of the two main factors – jobs and lifestyle – is most important entirely depends on the specific target group. In Chapters Five and Six, you can read an interview with Yvonne van Hest, programme director for Brainport Eindhoven Region's talent attraction efforts, which sheds much light on precisely this issue. She underscores that for the tech and IT people that they want to recruit to the region, the jobs they offer are the most important factor for talent attraction. It is the content of the jobs that matters most. However, for a city like Amsterdam, for example, that attracts more marketers and people in other 'creative' occupations, lifestyle factors may play a larger role.

In any case, what is clear is that *place matters*, and most likely it matters now more than ever. An increasing body of research suggests that economic growth is concentrating in larger urban regions and clusters of businesses where proximity and knowledge-sharing lead to innovation. So if talents cluster in one place, the local rate of economic development accelerates.[13]

This brings us to the main question of this book.

How can places attract and retain talent?

No doubt, cities, regions and countries need to work actively with activities and services to attract and retain talent, especially those that do not possess the more 'organic' attraction factors that places like London, Paris, Silicon Valley or Berlin do, for example.

---

13   Lucas in Florida et al. (2009) and Mortetti (2014)

This is what we call Talent Attraction Management.

Figure 1 outlines the aspects that a place needs to manage in order to be attractive for international talent,[14] in the context of the main overall aspects of place attractiveness for talents.

There is a range of framework conditions and enablers that the place needs to work actively with in order to be attractive to talent, such as influencing policies (e.g. immigration, tax policy), political climate (e.g. creating awareness of the need to be open to labour immigration), accessibility (e.g. physical and digital infrastructure) and education and research (e.g. schools, universities, lifelong learning).

What is Talent Attraction Management?

Talent Attraction Management is a holistic, integrated approach to efforts at the local, regional or national level aimed at attracting and retaining talents.[15]

We categorise Talent Attraction Management (TAM) in five different types of activities:

1. **Talent attraction** – such as marketing and recruitment activities
2. **Talent reception** – such as welcoming and soft landing activities
3. **Talent integration** – through social and professional networks, for example
4. **Talent reputation** – such as place and employer branding efforts and ambassador networks models
5. **Management of ecosystem** – stakeholder, network and project coordination

---

14 Inspired by Professor and HR guru David Ulrich, we take a holistic view when defining talent, which also makes it subjective, i.e. it is dependent on the needs of employers and regions. The definition is: talent = *competence commitment contribution*. In this formulation, 'competence' means that individuals have the knowledge, skills and values that are required for today and tomorrow. 'Commitment' means that employees work hard, putting the time in to do what they are asked to do, and giving their discretionary energy to the firm's success. 'Contribution' means that they are making a real difference through their work — finding meaning and purpose in it. Please read more here: http://bwl.univie.ac.at/fileadmin/user_upload/lehrstuhl_ind_en_uw/lehre/ss11/Sem_Yuri/JIM-talent.pdf.

15 Tendensor (2014)

One key notion is that successful talent attraction and retention depend on actively working with all five aspects of the Talent Attraction Management model. The model rests on the idea that each step reinforces the following steps. For example, the more effectively the attraction efforts are carried out, the more talents will need reception. As a result, there is an aspect of expectations management too, meaning that marketing activities need to be truthful and create sound expectations in relation to the subsequent steps

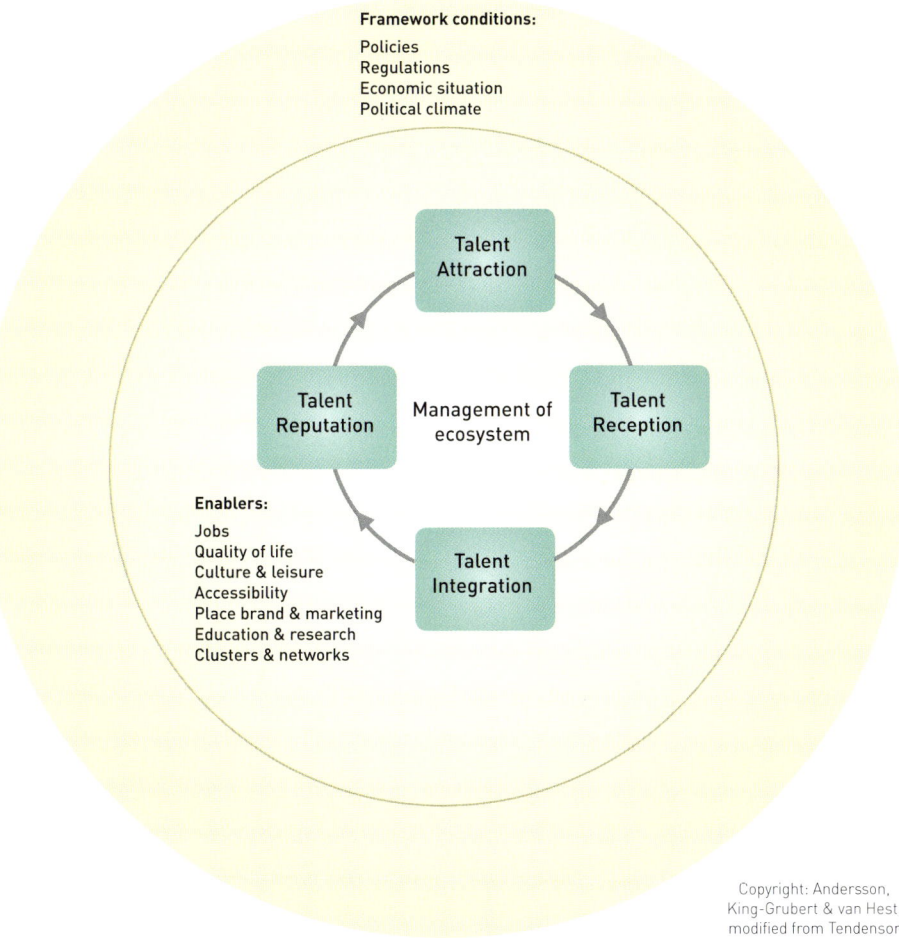

Figure 1: Talent Attraction Management

If we peel the onion, so to speak, we find the four cornerstones of Talent Attraction Management: attraction, reception, integration and reputation. These will be discussed in the next section.

(reception and integration of the talents) to be successful. An illustration is the Icelandic computer games company that brought every potential recruit over to Iceland for an interview, ideally during wintertime (as opposed to only doing phone interviews), just to make sure that the person in question would know what he or she said yes to.

In the same vein, the better the reception a person gets in the reception phase, the easier the integration will become in the subsequent phase. A positive reception and successful integration will help build the reputation of the place, as the talents will spread the word to friends and networks about its merits and qualities. The improved reputation will, in turn, make any attraction efforts easier and more successful.

Different stakeholders, such as public sector organisations, private employers and universities, typically carry out the four types of activities. In order to make sure that the region presents a coordinated and consistent marketing and service offer, management of the talent attraction ecosystem is also needed, as it forms the 'glue' that keeps the different parts of the TAM model together.

Having said that, countries, cities and regions can put emphasis on different steps where insufficiencies or weak links are identified. For example, a city may have a strong brand image and manage to attract a lot of talent without any proactive marketing efforts, but face difficulties welcoming or retaining them. In such cases, increased focus on reception and integration efforts may be needed. Conversely, a location that has efficient processes and efforts in place to ensure a good reception and integration but lacks a strong reputation may need to enhance their efforts to brand and market the location to international talent.

From a broader perspective, we fundamentally believe that an overriding objective of Talent Attraction Management is to improve conditions for *talent mobility* – so-called brain circulation. We argue that if all locations become better at all steps of the model outlined in this chapter, mobility would increase. For example, the better the reception a person gets when moving to a new place, the more positive the migration experience is perceived to be and – perhaps paradoxically – the more prone the person will be to move again. And the person will leave as a great ambassador for the place, and most likely recommend other internationals to go to the region they just left.

It is a team effort

When it comes to management of the talent attraction ecosystem, it is important to acknowledge the multi-stakeholder setting: many different stakeholders with different objectives, priorities and mandates need to be involved to make sure that a comprehensive and coordinated chain of services and activities can be supplied.

And let us be honest: often that means a lot of egos and logos need to work together, which is not easy to accomplish.

Managing the ecosystem is therefore often a matter of managing and coordinating organisations, networks, people and teams representing multiple place-based stakeholders. One cannot rely on one organisation managing and controlling the required processes in a traditional, hierarchal manner.

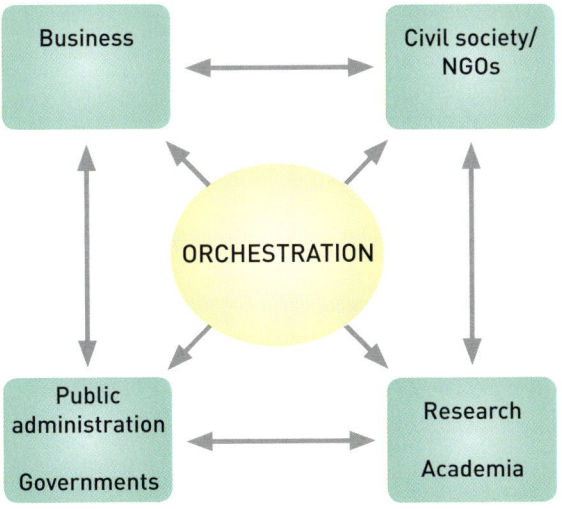

Source: Nordic Place Academy, 2016

Figure 2: Quadruple-helix multi-stakeholder setting of Talent Attraction Management In short, team efforts and collaborative leaderships are needed. We call this orchestration, which is a metaphor meant to signify the need for different stakeholders to work in a coordinated manner ('play the same musical score'), and that someone needs to take on the role ('the conductor') of making sure that that is the case. The role of civil society and NGOs should not be underestimated here. Social entrepreneurship can help tackle many of the needs talents have when it comes to welcoming, and social and professional integration. For example, if you succeed in involving the talent themselves in the service provision, understanding needs and designing services and support measures naturally become easier.

Instead, successful talent attraction and retention requires systemic management of an ecosystem of different public and private, and often also academic and societal stakeholders; this is known as quadruple-helix ('quad-helix') collaboration.

What skills do you need to manage and orchestrate this complex multi-stakeholder setting?

In a recent training session with many of the leading Talent Attraction Management entities in Europe, held by Nordic Place Academy, we asked the participants what skills you need as a talent attraction manager. This is their list:

- Connectivity
- Communications skills
- Lobby skills
- Project management
- Business-oriented
- Network management
- Open-minded
- Global thinker
- Marketing / Sales / PR / Social media
- HR & people skills
- Listening
- Diplomacy
- Strategic understanding
- Thinking outside the box
- Risk taker
- Change manager
- Fundraising

This is some list. Few individuals can master all of it; at the session, we characterised the individuals who work in this area as 'superheroes'.

One key conclusion was how important it is to get a team on board with a broad set of skills. In Chapter Five, we will discuss such organisational and management issues in more detail.

References

Beechler, S. & Woodward, I. C. (2009). The Global "War for Talent". *Journal of International Management* 15: 273-285.

Christopherson, S. & Michael, S. (1987). Flexible Specialization and Regional Industrial Agglomerations: The Case of the U.S. Motion Picture Industry. *Annals of the Association of American Geographers* 77(1): 104-117.

International Regions Benchmarking Consortium (2009). A Tale of Ten Cities: Attracting and Retaining Talent. Prepared for the 2nd Annual Meeting of the International Regions Benchmarking. http://www.internationalregions.org/Full-TalentReport.Pdf. Accessed September 23, 2016.

Izquierdo, M., Jimeno, J.F., & Lacuesta, A. (2015). Spain: From immigration to emigration. Banco de Espana.

Lucas, R. in Florida, R. (2009). *Who's Your City?: How the Creative Economy Is Making Where to Live the Most Important Decision of your Life*. New York: Basic Books.

Michaels, E., Handfield-Jones, H. & Axelrod, B. (2001). *The War for Talent*. Harvard Business Press.

Moretti, E. (2014). *The New Geography of Jobs*. Boston/New York: Marine Books.

Niedomysl, T. & Hansen H.K. (2010). What matters more for the decision to move: jobs versus amenities. *Environment and Planning A* 42: 1636-1649.

Nordic Place Academy (2016). *Handbook on Business Attraction Management for Cities and Regions*. http://placeacademy.com/publications/ Accessed September 23, 2016.

Tendensor (2014). *Handbook on Talent Attraction Management for Cities and Region*. http://tendensor.com/publications/ Accessed September 23, 2016.

Interview with Charlotte Mark, Microsoft

Managing director, Microsoft Development Center Copenhagen

A few words about Microsoft Development Center Copenhagen

Microsoft Development Center Copenhagen is based on an acquisition of the Danish company Navision, which happened in 2002. The Center counts 300 employees, mainly software engineers. Approximately 50 percent of our employees are of nationalities other than Danish and together they represent 43 different nationalities, with a majority from Poland, Ukraine and Romania.

Why does Microsoft Development Center Copenhagen need international talent?

We need international talent for two reasons. Firstly, it helps us understand different market needs, think out of the box and be more innovative. Putting 10 engineers with the same cultural background in a room together and asking them to solve a problem, their solution will simply not be as creative and innovative as that of a diverse workgroup. We need the diversity. Secondly, the demographic changes that we are facing – not only in Denmark but in most of Europe – makes it critical for Danish companies to be able to attract international talent.

How would you describe the value international talent brings to your organisation?

We develop software for the global market and must understand the different needs depending on geography, industry, etc. for our solutions to be attractive and useful for companies around the world. Bringing people together with diverse backgrounds results in different questions being asked and different solutions being considered, and increases our ability to create truly innovative solutions. This can only be achieved with a truly international team.

How do you recruit international talent to Denmark?

We have been recruiting internationally since 2005 and it is getting easier. We have also learned over time where to find the best technical universities and how to reach out to the relevant candidates. Microsoft's University Recruitment team travels around the world with all of Microsoft's open positions. This enables us to tap into great pools of talent. When it comes to more experienced candidates, we often use social media to get in contact with them and build a relation. The process of hiring an experienced candidate takes a long time because you have to warm them up to the idea of them moving to a new position in a new country, and that can actually take several months – sometimes years.

How important is the place brand, relative to the job, in the hiring process?

It depends on what kind of candidate we are looking for. For a college hire (typically without a family) the main focus is on the career opportunities, while the focus on place and living conditions comes as secondary. An experienced hire (4+ years of experience) focuses on a combination of both the job and the place – to them the place and living conditions are very important because they often have a family, and that raises questions like "can we live on one salary?", or "can our kids go to an international school?" and "what about a job for my spouse?". They are simply more concerned with the way of life than a college hire because they bring families with them. However, once they are here – the college hire and the experienced hire – the liveability of Denmark comes to mean a lot to both categories.

How do you practically manage to recruit internationally?

When hiring from around the world it is often difficult to bring in the candidates for an interview. Hence, we always do the initial screening through Skype. Once we have qualified the candidate we either fly them in or we set up a whole day with interviews in a particular country and fly out ourselves. That has proven very effective.

What do you see as your biggest recruitment challenge in the future?

Obviously the demographic changes that we see not only in Denmark but in Europe is going to continue to be a problem, and I think it is important that Danish companies really embrace the idea of recruiting internationally. There is such a shortage of engineers and scientists in Denmark in general, and there is an even bigger shortage when it comes to women with a STEM education (Science, Technology, Engineering and Mathematics). That is a serious challenge which may impact Denmark's competitiveness in the global market!

3 Talent Attraction Management in practice – The Copenhagen Case

As practitioners in this field, we have come across many inspirational initiatives from different cities, regions and countries aiming at attracting and retaining an international workforce. From different ways of doing recruitment missions to employer and place branding storytelling, digital platforms as well as apps to soft landing initiatives, the list of great concepts is getting longer and longer as new entities are entering the playing field with innovative approaches.

Throughout this book, we will refer to the most relevant ones we have come across. In this chapter, we will initially zoom in on one specific inspirational initiative, namely the development of the talent attraction and retention efforts of Copenhagen, as it is a vivid illustration of the TAM model and its holistic approach outlined in Chapter Two. The case also serves to illustrate the product portfolio use by Copenhagen – concrete, innovative tools and activities that help attract, receive and integrate international talent, that can inspire other locations.

Now, as two of the three authors at different and overlapping times have been actively involved in the Copenhagen talent efforts as both decision-makers and practitioners from the very beginning, let us start by offering the following disclaimer:

We would like to thank all of our international partners, who have given positive feedback on the strategy and activities of Copenhagen at different stages during the past five years. Personally, we do not consider our efforts to be best in class, but rather a long, exciting journey of learning and improving, making mistakes and continuously adapting to stakeholder needs and regional economic framework conditions. And getting to where Copenhagen is today within regional Talent Attraction Management (TAM) has been a team effort, so any and all kudos and credit go to all parties involved, not the authors in question.

Following the Copenhagen case, we will expand the discussion in Chapter Four, attempting to categorise best practices we have seen around the world (not just in Copenhagen) into recommendations of areas that we strongly suggest you consider as part of your overall TAM initiatives.

The Copenhagen case: From FDI to talent attraction

Copenhagen Capacity started looking into talent attraction activities in winter 2009-2010. As the official foreign direct investment agency of the Greater Copenhagen Capital region, the primary reason for the organisation's move into this area came from its clients, namely international investors. Back then (and still to this day) Copenhagen Capacity increasingly experienced that access to skilled labour was becoming one of the key decision-making factors when the international investor was choosing a region to launch new business activities. In the case of Copenhagen, this typically related to establishing a Scandinavian head office or sales office, as well as R&D or logistics facilities. Adding together the demographics forecasts of Denmark, with a severe future lack of highly skilled labour due to large proportions of individuals close to retirement age and low numbers entering their professional life in the coming years, the case was simple: something needed to be done. Not just to put more impetus into attracting international investors, but also to retain the overall competitiveness of the region and ensure the existing companies would not outsource core business functions, or even, in a worst case scenario, leave completely due to lack of access to a talent pool.

Copenhagen Capacity had not come across the TAM model when they were considering how to solve the future talent gap of the region. The more public and private organisations Copenhagen Capacity approached, the more complex the area seemed to be. For example, considering the right government entity to discuss the overall strategy with, the list included, among others, the Ministry of Employment, the Ministry of Integration, the Ministry of Business and Growth, the Ministry of Foreign Affairs and the Ministry of Higher Education and Science – just to name the most relevant ones. You could even easily add the Ministry of Culture and a few more. In addition, it seemed that many different municipalities in the region were doing great things, some overlapping and others completely unaware of what their neighbours were doing. Consequently, the subsequent knowhow and best practice was lost at the border between zip codes, with the irony that such borders typically are completely unknown to the target group of international talent.

The Copenhagen Capacity methodology only came to life when the flow in the decision-making processes of the international talent itself became the cornerstone of the strategy, requiring an understanding of the almost mini lifecycle stages, from initial interest in relocating abroad to returning back to the original home region or embarking on a new international venture somewhere else.

As such, the strategy ended up being very similar to the TAM model presented in Chapter Two. The Copenhagen model had four stages, *attraction*, *welcoming*, *living* and *leaving*.

Attraction

Copenhagen and Denmark often appear in top 10 rankings for easy of doing business, liveability, environmental conscience and even happiness. Consequently, one might imagine that Copenhagen has a talent brand appeal by default. The reality was and is that this alone does not secure a steady natural inflow of international talents. If nobody knows you exist or where you are located, these statistics do not matter. As stated in Chapter One, Copenhagen is often thought to be the Capital of Sweden by internationals, and the language spoken is also a matter of mystery for some – a small country in an odd corner of the world, how should you know! In short, almost disregarding how cool or vibrant your region is, branding is required and the story you have needs to get out beyond your borders. Copenhagen Capacity realised this from the very beginning and defined talent attraction activities as a centrepiece in their strategy.

Welcoming

If Copenhagen were to be very successful in its attraction activities and its international marketing works, literally thousands and thousands of talents would be eager to relocate to the region. But if these talents cannot get work or spouse visas, only limited housing is available, there are no international schools for the kids or it is burdensome to a bank account or a social security number, then all the attraction activities might not be completely wasted, but close to it. The stakeholders in Copenhagen realised this from the beginning. Furthermore, it is important to make sure that all internationals feel extremely welcomed throughout their stay in the region. Yet in practical terms, the welcoming period is defined from the person's initial interest in the place to that very first day at work, university or even at school for the children, where all these practicalities should be in order.

Living

All other continuing "welcoming" activities are integrated in what came to be termed 'living'. It is commonly accepted that most expat assignments fail not because the expat is not performing at or happy with his/her job; rather, most fail because the accompanying family is not happy and well integrated into society. This integration can take different forms depending on cultural background. In some cases, the accompanying spouse (he/she) may want to continue a professional career in this new country, and the primary living activities will be targeted towards just that. Tailoring the CV to a local context, setting up mentor networks, attending spouse career fairs, and considering entrepreneurial start-up options are some of the typical activities within this scope. In other cases, the accompanying spouse is quite comfortable taking a sabbatical year looking after the family or pursuing other interests from sports to non-profit activities. In such situations, the living activities should be more focused towards social and cultural integration.

Leaving

Last but definitely not least, the Copenhagen framework offers a variation on most talent attraction and retention activities – a 'leaving' phase. At first, this may seem a bit counterproductive. The first thing that comes to mind is a puzzled reaction: are you really trying to make sure the expats leave? The answer is rather the contrary. By default, international talents are notoriously international and mobile. So even though a company and the region would often benefit from having the talent for a long and continuous period, one must acknowledge that by many standards the assignment is temporary. Unless of course there are other private reasons – romantic ones – where the expat decides to stay because he or she has met someone during the assignment, or even originally came because they met someone from the area elsewhere and moved back with them. In the business of talent attraction and retention, we may as well be honest, and say that this has a significant importance. At some point, most expats will either miss their home country or alternatively be motivated by a new international experience in another region. In this case, there are a few things to consider. One is simply to say goodbye. Another is to add a thank you for the value the talent created, while he or she was working. Or – and this is the 'leaving' phase of Copenhagen's programme – you can work very closely with the person in question, making him or her an official ambassador of the region, and thereby continuing the relationship with them during the time he or she spends in the new place. Chances are that since the person was originally recruited to a company located in Greater Copenhagen because of certain skills and industry knowledge, he or she will engage in a network in the new or the home region with similar professionals, matching the target group of Greater Copenhagen.

Adding the missing link – a regional talent strategy

When Copenhagen Capacity initiated its talent activities, they found that the ecosystem within the talent area was not working together enough. At the same time, many of the knowledge-intensive companies and institutions within the regional business strongholds found it difficult to attract and retain enough of the most talented individuals, as the regional talent pool was not able to meet the market demand. As such, the organisation took the initiative to manage and orchestrate the ecosystem by developing a new strategy for attracting and retaining more talented internationals in the Copenhagen Region for the period of 2014-2017. Ultimately, the strategy identified 10 key initiatives within talent attraction and retention for the region to work on together across the private and public sectors. In the process, most relevant stakeholders participated, not just to develop the strategy, but also to take ownership of the execution of the strategy and align who needs to do what for the region to succeed long-term.

The 10 initiatives may serve as inspiration to other regions across the world. They are written as an invitation to international talents in their journey towards the region:

Initiative 1 – We will guide you to job openings in Copenhagen. With the Cluster Career Portals, we will create a single point of entry to all career opportunities in our strong regional clusters. Finding the right job in exciting business sectors has never been easier.

Initiative 2 – We will empower your career in Copenhagen. With the Cluster Campaigns, we will ensure that jobseekers are exposed to the many opportunities our strong regional clusters have to offer.

Initiative 3 – Copenhagen will win you over. With the Plug 'n' Play CPH marketing texts we will ensure that the reasons our international talent have for choosing Copenhagen become known to our future international talent.

Initiative 4 – We will expand your opportunities in Copenhagen. With the small- to medium-sized enterprises (SME) Referral Program, we will bridge the gap between international talent and regional SMEs and make even more job and career opportunities available to international talent.

Initiative 5 – We will make it easy to get information on Copenhagen. With the Information Fast Track package, we will make it easier for international talents to make an informed decision on choosing Copenhagen as their next career and living destination.

Initiative 6 – We will persuade you to return to Copenhagen. With the Return to Copenhagen initiative, we will gather existing offers and develop new services so that returning to Copenhagen becomes the obvious choice for international talents.

Initiative 7 – We will provide you with resources. With the Copenhagen Talent Charter, we will develop guarantees to international talents and their accompanying families such as job interviews for accompanying spouses and international students.

Initiative 8 – We will give you a key to our culture. With the Copenhagen Season Pass, we will provide international talent with inexpensive access to the sports clubs and cultural activities in the Capital Region.

Initiative 9 – We will make relocating to Copenhagen easy. With the accommodation and housing initiative, we will improve upon existing accommodation options, and develop and deliver new types of flexible housing possibilities for international talent.

Initiative 10 – We will make your voice heard. With our Expat Panel and Copenhagen Talent Summit, we will make sure that the needs and wishes of international talents are kept firmly on the national agenda.

As a result of this regional talent strategy, the management of the ecosystem within talent attraction and retention in the Greater Copenhagen region has significantly improved and all key initiatives are now coordinated, both strategically and operationally. Although it is difficult to quantify the value of this, the positive effect is evident when you talk to the various organisations involved.

The product portfolio: Concrete tools catering to international talent

Initially, Copenhagen Capacity was involved in everything from offering Danish language courses to planning and executing marketing campaigns all over the world. In the process, the organisation learned a lot, but admittedly it also needed to identify its core value-adding activities to optimise resources and results.

The key question of who should be doing what was raised throughout the development of the regional talent strategy, as the various stakeholders got to know each other very well and built both a high level of knowledge and trust in their collaboration. Particularly, Copenhagen Capacity, the municipality of Copenhagen and the Confederation of Danish Industries (DI Global Talent) found a way to split the primary roles of attraction and retention. With the launch of the International House in Copenhagen by the municipality, all soft landing and welcoming activities for international talents has found is natural and physical home, leaving Copenhagen Capacity to carve out its niche in attraction and retention directly related to job creation. Likewise, DI – as the biggest employer organisation in Denmark – could focus even more on lobbying for the best possible framework conditions for companies.

Again, for inspiration to others, we provide a list of some of the services and products from the Copenhagen portfolio.

Toolbox to improve employer place branding
This toolbox was created to empower companies' recruitment of international professionals with marketing materials highlighting what life is like as an expat and employee in Denmark, thereby combining employer and place branding. The Toolbox is a complement to a company's existing recruitment efforts towards international workers. It contains free videos, images, infographics and articles in English, which tell future employees about living and working in Denmark. The materials can, for example, introduce the future employees to the Danish work culture and management style. They also give a picture of the communities where the new employee and his/her accompanying family will be living. All materials are in English and available in several formats, which can easily be adapted to the corporate visual identity of the given company.

Recruitment campaigns online and offline

The Talent Attraction campaigns tell the story of Greater Copenhagen's exciting business environment and of career opportunities within the target groups' academic field. The campaigns target those who are not necessarily actively seeking new jobs among international specialists working within cleantech, life science as well as information and communications technology (ICT). For example, campaigns have included marketing in scientific journals, through professional organisations on LinkedIn, via alumni networks, at conferences and on other platforms where international specialists might seek information about their field of study. The campaigns highlight the Danish work culture, including the opportunity to combine career and family life, while presenting Danish companies and their specific job openings in Greater Copenhagen.

App for international recruitment

The 'Move to DK' app is a practical checklist for international talents considering Denmark. By sending the free app to potential employees, a HR department can save resources and provide top service to their future employees. Move to DK is a mobile application for phones and tablets, which helps companies in Denmark in attracting international employees by simplifying the relocation process. It serves as a step-by-step checklist and a one-point entry to the many websites and authorities to contact regarding relocation to Denmark to live and work. This app is organised around three stages in the decision-making process of internationals considering relocation: research, preparing and settling in. It answers many of the practical questions that international talents would otherwise contact their company's HR department for help with.

Company Challenge

The Company Challenge is a service for businesses in Denmark which allow companies to recruit newly-educated employees with international skills, as well as to work long-term to attract, retain and develop skilled staff. With the Company Challenge, Copenhagen Capacity selects a group of international students for an intensive day at the premises of a company in the region. The students, who are selected to match the company's specific needs, solve a case based on a challenge the company is currently facing. By working in real time with the company and getting to pitch their solution to company representatives, the students present the company with the opportunity to identify unique talents for future interviewing, employment and talent pipeline. As such, the company gets the opportunity to handpick the best talents and strengthen the company's reputation as a great workplace to the target group of international talents already in the region.

Go International

If a company in the region has export ambitions, Copenhagen Capacity can offer them the 'Go International' concept. The company is assigned a consultant identified by Copenhagen Capacity with significant knowledge of the language and market conditions in his/her home country, who can help the company reach new markets and export targets. Alongside their employment, the new employee will participate in a free training course at MBA level at Copenhagen Business School. The program will further strengthen the employee's sales and export competences – and the company's bottom line.

Youth Goodwill Ambassador Corps

Twenty years ago Copenhagen Capacity founded – in partnership with the tourist organisation Wonderful Copenhagen – an ambassador programme for members of the Danish C-level diaspora who are eager to give back, pro bono, to their original home region. The ambassadors serve as Greater Copenhagen's marketers and network connectors in relevant (more than 30) international markets. When launching its talent initiatives, Copenhagen Capacity was inspired by this goodwill notion and decided to run a youth ambassador programme for international students. The premise: Why should Danish companies go to China (or any other relevant market) to do employer branding and attract talent, when that (in this example Chinese) talent is already studying at the local university in Denmark? And when that university is doing international marketing, why not make the storytelling much more authentic and trustworthy by having an international student from the given target region in question share his/her experiences of studying and living in Denmark? In addition, by launching a programme for international students, giving them a VIP experience of Denmark, perhaps they would not only be happy to share their story, but also to stay longer and seek job opportunities in Denmark at the end of their studies.

After they apply through the Danish host university – partners in the initiative – the international students are appointed 'Youth Goodwill Ambassador of Denmark'. They participate in Danish corporate, culture and competence building workshops, attaining fun and unique insights into the Danish society at large and access to leading industries and businesses. They carry out marketing events all over the world, leveraging their access to the universities of their place of origin. This model has served well with the introduction of a marketing grant, where the international students pitch their creative ideas on how to make a successful promotion. As a result, the best applications receive funding to cover project costs and strategic guidance to implement the concept. The Ambassadors are also active in the international press; Copenhagen has found a way to make them the centrepiece of the storyline, thereby providing a win–win situation. The Ambassadors receive personal branding opportunities (name/picture in the news) and the location (in this case, Denmark) receives targeted publicity that is personalised with a positive case. So far, more than 35 countries have picked up stories about Denmark as a student destination based on the work of the Youth Ambassadors. With the Youth Goodwill Ambassador Corps, Copenhagen has also found a way to adopt a more personal peer-to-peer approach to digital marketing. The Youth Ambassadors utilise their activities on social media to participate in study abroad forums in their home countries, responding to questions about studying in Denmark. They offer personal experience examples and give advice on topics ranging from submitting university applications to where to find the best café in the local neighbourhood.

The programme is increasing its focus on retention of international students in the region after completion of their degree. Copenhagen Capacity thus acts as the matchmaker between the international student and the companies in the region – who often are not aware of each other's existence.

International House Copenhagen
Moving on to the public administration of soft landing activities, International House Copenhagen serves as a one-stop shop, a physical entity for all public registration processes and access to all relevant organisations

working with international talent in the Greater Copenhagen Region. The open house facility deals with coming to and settling in requirements, encompassing administrative needs (getting a personal identity number, health card etc.) as well as providing efforts related to social and professional networks to international talent in the region, helping them to build their career, develop professionally and feel at home.

From Copenhagen to the rest of the world

Many places around the world have a strong brand and positive brand associations, as well as perceptions that link their marketing activities back to the brand. However, we dare to argue that many places need to develop a stronger 'employer place brand' of their region, that is, specifically as a career destination. Copenhagen Capacity and its partners have – in our humble opinion – proven to be leaders within talent attraction and retention on a Nordic scale. As a foreign direct investment agency, all activities of the Copenhagen Capacity talent department must relate to job creation. Consequently, from starting out with orchestrating and optimising the ecosystem through the development of the regional talent strategy – and in the process being involved in a multitude of activities – Copenhagen Capacity has found its niche with core products directly aimed at companies with a competence need. The organisation understands that you cannot attract without retention and soft landing activities, and you must work closely with participating partners, who are often better equipped to provide value within these areas.

Moreover, Copenhagen Capacity has found ways to engage and mobilise both employers and talent through different initiatives, thereby ensuring that activities are demand-driven and that they harness the creative and innovative power that can stem from making stakeholders co-creators of activities.

Ranging from tools for co-branding with employers to the goodwill ambassador participatory approach to talent engagement, we believe Copenhagen Capacity is a very relevant case for other regions to explore – especially when first moving into regional talent attraction and retention. It is particularly relevant for those readers who would like to go all in, and work on all elements of the TAM model outlined in Chapter Two. However, there are many other great inspirational cases, initiatives and methodologies from other regions. We would like to bring these to light in the following chapters. All cases can be found in further detail in Appendix Two, starting with our suggested strategic recommendations for successful Talent Attraction Management.

Interview with Paul Evans, INSEAD

Emeritus professor of organisational behaviour, INSEAD

Why has talent attraction become so important?

There are three reasons why talent attraction is important. First of all, we have moved into the knowledge society and are becoming increasingly dependent on talent for productivity and growth. Secondly, because of the European countries' demographical challenge, many "grey-hairs" have retired, so we are in high need of new influx to the labour force. But the third and most important reason why talent attraction is important is the fact that we have severe skill gaps in Europe. The reality is that our educational system in Europe is not particularly well adapted for employability. The youngsters study something different from what the labour market demands. That problem is going to become more acute due to the technological changes in society.

What makes a winner in talent attraction?

Using our data from the Global Talent Competitiveness Index (CTCI) and other research on this issue, we have been trying to figure out what makes a winner. There are different elements that make a country attractive. Language is important; if you cannot speak the same language, you cannot work together. It is absolutely fundamental. Also, cities must pay attention to creating an attractive lifestyle – especially for young people. You have to work with countries and cities to address these lifestyle factors.

You have more mobility around the world and more young people are travelling. Until 2000, people mostly wanted to go to the US – no doubt that it is the most attractive country for international skills. Many essential factors are fulfilled in the US, such as: English language, you have regions with attractive career opportunities, attractive lifestyles, a finely-tuned educational system, high salaries and meritocratic management practices. The US would definitely be on top of the index if it focused only on talent attraction.

The Nordic Region scores particularly high in the GTCI – why is that? What is the region's value proposition, to your mind?

Management practices also attract people. Nordics have an intangible asset here. I call it meritocratic empowerment, meaning that the Nordics are good at believing in people, letting them learn more and thereby, grow more. If you look around the world at who is good at developing people on the job, it is the Nordic region. This is something that can be marketed and which people find to be particularly attractive. The way I have headlined this in the past is: "if you want to live the American Dream – don't go the US, go to the Nordics". There are many parts of the world where the companies and governments are extremely hierarchical – where you follow orders and instructions. The Nordics have a very meritocratic culture, where good individuals will be recognised.

Are there any big traps you should avoid in relation to talent attraction?

Fast integration should be avoided. At the moment, the line of thought is focused on how to help people integrate quickly and thereby retain them. I think this is indeed a false assumption. The reality is that you do not need people to integrate into society; you need them to stay for three to five years. You bring somebody from e.g. Italy to Denmark, because you offer him or her, if not a high salary, then a great lifestyle and personal growth and development. When they then return to Italy, they will act as an ambassador of Denmark, due to the memories and contacts they have obtained. They may connect their company in Italy to their Danish counterparts, they may set up their own businesses and establish a Danish branch.

The striking thing is that these mobile people appear to be innovative and entrepreneurial talents. I see an interesting paradox here: we are trying to attract people from foreign countries, but if we want to keep them here, we also need to encourage our own citizens to go and study abroad because we need the innovative input of true internationals. I have a vision of building a world of brain-circulation!

Is the key locus for Talent Attraction changing from the national level to a city/regional effort? If so, why?

To deal with these challenges, you need a close collaboration between the state on the one hand and business on the other – and collaborations with educational institutions. Our prediction is that these activities will move progressively from countries to cities. In our GTCI results you see that the leading countries are mostly small countries like Singapore, which is a city-state. Switzerland and Denmark are also small states. If you look at the US on a city level, you see another point of view in terms of talent attraction. The activity will move progressively towards cities due to the need to be able to connect a lot of actors while being agile, in order to build up your specific value proposition.

4 Strategic Recommendations for Successful Talent Attraction Management

Let us seek to lay out some overall strategic recommendations that stem from the many regional talent attraction entities we have talked to and researched. In short, what is there to learn from the best in the field?

In this chapter, you can expect to find not only inspiration from how the talent attraction and retention business is run by others, but also a more hands-on approach to take your talent attraction ambitions and activities forward. The focus here is on specific methodologies, strategies and tools that we suggest you consider when optimising your location's efforts within Talent Attraction Management. Some of the methodologies used by leading Talent Attraction Management regions globally score highly in our view due to their innovative and even disruptive approaches, as opposed to years of well-run public–private strategy. However, the latter should not be underestimated, as a focused, long-term and inclusive approach has proven to yield great results. These examples and recommendations are not meant to serve as one-size-fits-all solutions, but rather for you to select the most suitable methodologies and strategies, and seasoned with your unique mix of local strengths and ambitious goals, create your own recipe for success.

We will outline five strategic recommendations which we have developed based on the assessment of the most promising approaches in an innovative talent attraction scheme. The five recommendations are:

1. Engaging talents as ambassadors
2. Engaging employers
3. Interregional talent sharing: from foes to friends
4. Finding your niche: competitive advantage and authenticity
5. Disrupting and innovating to differentiate

Engaging talents as ambassadors

Talent Attraction Management entities need to realise that every aspect of a talent's journey is important. Talent mobility needs to be embraced and there are plenty of opportunities to make each step a great experience for the talent and an undeniable place branding opportunity for the location. Several of the early adopters in talent attraction have realised that involving talent and empowering people to contribute to the community can form a long-lasting bond with the target group, leading to long-term benefits for the region. They have found ways to engage the international talent in various branding activities, ultimately creating a good reputation for the location as a place for talents to thrive in.

There are multiple reasons why we claim that engaging talent is proven to be one of the best strategies. Firstly, personal peer-to-peer recommendations and honest storytelling are credible marketing tools. An ambassador network is a smart tool for marketing the location to current and previous internationals. Secondly, talent engagement extends the expat lifecycle to the phase after leaving the location as it embraces talent mobility, and stays connected to people. Thirdly, ambassador networks keep the public and private sector connected to the talent agenda at large and can therefore positively influence the public's and decision-makers' views on immigration and labour market openness. Finally, talent engagement enables co-branding and co-creation.

The best practice example of talent engagement strategies that we advocate for are ambassador and alumni networks. Through these programmes, the creative power and global outreach of international talent can be harnessed.

The following points introduce successful global examples of ambassador networks along with our recommendations on how to improve this aspect of your own work.

A. Include talent in the equation. As outlined in Chapter Three, Copenhagen has developed the Youth Goodwill Ambassador Corps as a global network of 500+ talented international students who study or have studied in Denmark. Inviting talent to take part in discussions and be part of official promotional campaigns not only provides innovative solutions but also enables ownership of these activities, since they address real issues and have real consequences.

Chile enrols all entrepreneurs taking part in the Start-Up Chile programme in an alumni network upon graduation, creating a channel to reach their home countries and communities. The unique part of this particular case is that all participants become part of 'history in the making', telling a great story about Chile, positively impacting the local community and creating a 'great ambassadors network' on a global scale.

B. Involve talent in marketing, networks and events – at home and abroad. Again, through the Youth Goodwill Ambassador Corps, the international students carry out marketing events for Copenhagen and Denmark all over the world, leveraging their access to universities in their home regions. The ambassadors are also active in the international press, providing a personalised story about their own experiences in the location, which leads to personal branding (it is their name/picture in the news) and location branding (Denmark). Based on the work of the Youth Ambassadors and with more than 35 countries covering stories on how Denmark can serve as a student destination, the model seems to be a success.

Start-up Chile's alumni partner with local embassies around the globe to facilitate free meet-ups and events in order to promote the programme and create connections to potential talent, often free of charge. By taking the community-based approach, Start-Up Chile has managed to eliminate nearly all marketing and promotion costs, and through co-created marketing efforts earned itself significant international exposure. This has helped ensure the attraction of the critical mass required to build a viable start-up community.

C. Digitally adopt a more personalised and community-based approach. This approach is about shifting from a one-way (mass) communication approach to a more personalised, two-way approach, in order to engage international talents more closely and build stronger links with them.

The Youth Goodwill Ambassador Corps, in Copenhagen, provides an illustration of adopting a more personal approach to digital marketing. Social media allows the youth ambassadors to be active in study abroad forums in their home countries, engaging in Q&A sessions about studying in Denmark. This exchange offers opportunities to share personal experiences on Copenhagen and Denmark while also sharing advice on various topics ranging from the university application process to everyday life in the city.

D. Build experience. When creating a talent attraction programme, remember who your end user is. Building an experience around programmes such as Start-Up Chile attracts people with different backgrounds and ambitions. If managed cleverly, it can create a community experience revolving around – among other things – the opportunity to make history. The value of this approach should not be underestimated, particularly when considering that experience is one of the main attraction factors for the millennial generation.

E. Encourage international presence. Tel Aviv, Israel represents yet another perspective on ambassador engagement. An ambassador can offer a credible testimony of the attractiveness and the competitive edge of the place. The ambassadors' own personal networks can enrich the social capital of the place and lead to fruitful new global business relations. By fostering the risk-taking culture, entrepreneurs and talent in Tel Aviv are encouraged to test their entrepreneurial potential in foreign markets. Many have been successful in growing their business by setting up another office in e.g. Silicon Valley, while maintaining a head office in Tel Aviv, thereby promoting their home country/city and establishing new contacts between home and new markets.

Engage employers

Engaging companies or employers in governance and the planning, development and execution of activities is a good way of making them more demand-driven and often even co-financed. Another benefit is that involving employers to a larger extent helps ensure that they take ownership of talent-related activities, engage in the processes and become ambassadors of the place brand.

The best practice examples involve companies from a very early stage in the development process of building tools and initiatives. In some cases, these best practice examples invite company representatives to be part of both steering committees on a senior management level, and project work groups on a project manager level.

Engage companies early in the process

One of the pioneers in Europe has been Brainport Development, which has involved companies in working groups and activities from the very beginning to make sure that all efforts are demand-driven. Brainport also does this from a corporate branding perspective: getting the regional 'multi-helix' players more engaged by telling their stories to the world. It is based on peer-to-peer marketing, thereby reaching a broader worldwide network by sharing the stories of the region's different ambassadors, both companies and talent.

Place and employer branding through cohesive storytelling

Another example of close involvement of firms is how Copenhagen Capacity's Talent Attraction Denmark toolbox was developed. As introduced in Chapter Three, the toolbox provides companies with the right story of the region – with respect to both the dynamic business environment at large, and the social aspects of living in the region. The toolbox was tested with and by companies, ranging from coding the specs to prototype and subsequent updates. The same process was used when developing the subsequent campaign platform.

Similar in concept is the Brainport TalentBOX. It is the online portal for worldwide tech and IT talents to find jobs, knowledge and networks. It functions as a marketing and information portal as well as a tool for recruitment and engagement with the target group of international talent, facilitating a dialogue between employers and international talent under the place branding umbrella Brainport Eindhoven Region.

Foster networks and interaction between companies and talent

Tampere in Finland introduced the TreStart network, which is an innovation platform that brings together companies and the unemployed, where both parties sit down together to look for opportunities to create new jobs. The concept is based on an ambition to engage 1000 highly educated unemployed people and 150 companies by 2017 and create 300 jobs.

Inclusive boards of directors to follow what companies need

Some organisations have struggled to run international recruitment events due to lack of company participation. A company's participation can be incredibly powerful, for instance by sending a representative to interview the candidates and make the format a success.

Montréal has found a setup that is so valuable to companies that they finance a significant proportion of its talent attraction events. The Board of Directors of Montréal International includes, aside from public sectors representatives, members from leading industries in the region. In this way it is ensured that both worlds work together on a common goal and that both are accountable for the strategic activities carried out. In addition, the inclusion of private stakeholders ensures that the activities carried out by Montréal International are connected to the actual needs of the market economy. In the case of recruitment missions, this means following the actual needs of the companies involved in the process.

Social Media

Engaging with the community and sharing quality content via social media can be a great way to co-brand companies and locations, as well as enhance dialogue between employers and international talent.

Stockholm Business Region (SBR) embraced this strategy in particular by creating a Twitter account called "Move to Stockholm". On a weekly basis, the account is handed to a new tech firm to host or 'curate' the account. Guidelines have been developed by SBR in close dialogue with the firms, which encourage them to share open positions, as well as insights into their work content and culture and life in Stockholm. The account also encourages other users to post under the hashtag #Movetostockholm whenever relevant.

The Tampere region and the dedicated Talent Tampere Network brings together employers and international talents, helping to find existing services for both these parties. For example, there is a LinkedIn community called "Linking Bright Business with Internationals", where companies interested in internationalisation can get help from the Talent Tampere Network. And the Tampere region itself will benefit from the work that is done to attract and retain more international talents.

Interregional talent sharing: From foes to friends

Recently, more and more locations arrive at what one could say is a very simple conclusion: in the world of talent mobility and the inevitable talent competition, it simply makes much more sense to cooperate rather than fight for the same talent. Optimising regional collaboration harbours great potential in terms of learning from one another, jointly influencing policy advocacy and boosting economic growth by making sure that talents find their way to where they are most needed. The most recent and inspiring illustration of this is offered by Berlin and Bizkaia.

Bizkaia:talent is a founding member of the European Regional Talent Mobility Network, which seeks to unite European regions in sharing talent amongst themselves and in branding a bigger region of opportunities to non-European markets. This network embraces talent mobility, building a regional platform that will enable talent to move successfully within the region, rather than choosing to leave for more distant locations.

Berlin, on the other hand, develops its talent sharing networks based on a specific talent group i.e. the entrepreneurs. Berlin takes part in pilot programmes with New York and Tel Aviv on entrepreneurial ecosystem collaboration, enabling entrepreneurial talent to freely move between the locations and plug into the local ecosystem for a specific period of time.

A successful TAM strategy is without doubt an inclusive one. Local governments, private companies, academia and talents contribute unique perspectives and resources to the development of TAM activities. Building partnerships in creating and delivering talent attraction activities ensures their relevance, as well as the support and ownership of the parties included. This augurs well for the result of those activities. In the world of talent mobility, some locations have been innovative in building partnerships with international partners in foreign countries to address talent shortages in their respective ecosystems. We consider Montréal to be amongst the best in class examples.

Montréal International works closely with local companies under their international recruitment missions programme. The partnership works so well that the companies decided to co-finance it. To make sure that the recruitment conducted in foreign countries/cities with the French- or Spanish-speaking target group, such as France or Barcelona (Spain), is aligned with the local agenda, the government of Québec makes sure all agreements are in place in good time. France is the country where most of the recruitment missions take place and where most talents are sourced. The French government actively supports the collaboration with the government of Québec, and has signed an agreement that facilitates the exchange of workers between the two regions. It is interesting to note that France supports talent circulation even though the country sees talent shortages; their gain is that it helps ensure that its young talents receive relevant international work experience and get an opportunity to learn English. For other countries, collaborating with Montréal's missions has presented an opportunity to alleviate unemployment of highly skilled talent.

Find your niche: Competitive advantage and authenticity

One of the aspects highlighted by some of the locations presented in this book as frontrunners in the talent attraction area is the strong focus on authenticity. Places like Chile and Austin explicitly emphasise the importance of staying true to the spirit of the location or community in their strategies and activities as the recipe for success, while Berlin for instance leverages its cheap living costs and creative vibe in attracting the brightest entrepreneurs. Being authentic should be understood as identifying the unique qualities of your place, be it city or region, and by the coordinated efforts of stakeholders involved in strategy formation, making sure these become embedded in the broader talent attraction strategy.

Authenticity leads to a focused strategy based on your location's strongholds and ambitions, the unique place offering and finding your niche. Based on best practice global examples, the points below follow our recommendations on how to improve this aspect in your own work.

Focus on particular skills groups, target markets or countries with a cultural/linguistic affinity

To name a few examples, Start-up Chile focuses on attracting start-up talent, Brainport Eindhoven on tech and IT talent, Montréal on primarily French-speaking talent, Bizkaia on those with a cultural bond to the region and Copenhagen on three main cluster sectors (ICT, life science and cleantech, and even more specifically, gaming within ICT). As concluded from our research, targeted approaches bring many advantages in terms of impact and cost-efficiency. In addition, a focused approach sends a clear message to the international talent, which for them can usually mean a simplified process with regards to relocation services, and for the TAM entities, a higher probability that companies will co-finance activities.

Simplify procedures and processes to get an edge
Just as companies can compete with a superior service level, locations can compete by providing high-quality services to international talent. For example, when attracting and retaining international talent, immigration procedures can prove to be a serious bottle-neck. Simplifying the immigration and soft landing procedures is not only essential to achieving a real success in TAM, but it can also be the best selling point you could ask for. Several countries have streamlined procedures to attract international talent.

New Zealand, for example, has set up a series of immigration procedures focusing on target groups that can bring value to business and society, the most innovative and eye-catching being a Global Impact Visa. This visa aims to attract 'solvers of global megatrends' to the country. Canada has created a special Start-Up Visa, to some extent taking advantage of flawed immigration policies in the US and other countries that at the time did not accommodate for international talents and entrepreneurs, forcing them to look for opportunities elsewhere. Chile is of course a case in point too, offering equity-free capital in addition to a one-year work visa for entrepreneurs without the bureaucracy behind the processes. Or why not offer virtual immigration? This is precisely what Estonia has done (read more in the next section, and in Chapter Six).

A visa targeted at a particular group of interest to your ecosystem can help achieve results in a pilot programme phase, without influencing the entire immigration system just yet.

Disrupt and innovate to differentiate

For those who are in the early stages of developing talent attraction strategies, or those trying to adapt existing activities to best practice examples, disruption and innovation to differentiate will be a particularly valid point. We argue that in order to foster innovation and economic growth in today's economy, not only do policies need to be adjusted, but people also need to be empowered and connected, as they are the real driving force behind the creation of unique place offerings. The competition is increasing, not only in terms of who is doing what, but also who is doing it best. The internationally mobile target group struggles more and more to identify the uniqueness of a given location. In this context, the next differentiator – and winner in an increasingly crowded market – will be the location that can best create awareness of themselves through a disruptive approach, along with an experience and/or community people want to be part of. The great disruptor on a global scale is of course the Start-Up Chile programme, but more examples exist. Austin, Texas has developed a music festival – South-by-Southwest – into a film and interactive festival, creating a unique combination of events and happenings that put the city on the map and attract a global audience of music, film and start-up talent. Estonia was the first country to introduce an e-residency programme, both attracting talents and sparking global media interest. Jönköping in Sweden made a web shop with free service products for talent considering moving to the city (read more in Chapter Six).

Being innovative and disruptive in your goals can be the best selling point for your location, helping attract talent from around the world. It can also create great value locally, as your domestic talent will not only want to become part of the unprecedented activities, but also help to co-create the brand by taking an active part in the ecosystem.

The recommendation is therefore clear: initiate a creative process to identify a disruptive approach to talent attraction, possibly by engaging a group of international and local talents in the co-creation process. The best innovators will be the future winners.

5 How to organise for Talent Attraction Management

As the competition for talent among cities and regions heats up, the required level of sophistication from the organisations delivering talent attraction and retention services continues to increase. This puts further emphasis on having the right organisational structure in place, as well as the alignment of the organisations providing the TAM services.

In this chapter, we discuss how to optimise the organisational structure of entities providing talent attraction services, as well as how funding and governance models can be put in place to support this structure. This also includes considering public–private partnerships, leveraging the activities of both parties, which creates an outcome that is bigger than the sum of the individual activities. Furthermore, we will share our experience in managing change processes in a local and regional setting derived from multiple projects in Europe and beyond. Thereby, we wish to provide a simple step-by-step guide to implement your strategy and activities following the inspiration and subsequent optimisation that this book hopefully provides.

Organisational structure to optimise talent attraction and retention

During our study of TAM organisations around the world,[16] we have come to identify five models of organisation. These are conceptualised as follows:

- A. The public sector-driven model
- B. The market- and sponsor-driven model
- C. The division of work model
- D. The network model
- E. The talent attraction arena-centric model

---

16 Tendensor (2014)

Hybrids of these models exist, therefore those listed should not be considered as fixed and mutually exclusive, nor should the overview above be regarded as an exhaustive list.

As most TAM entities are funded heavily by public means and/or publicly managed, we find that independent of the model chosen, two main challenges for the public sector exist:

1. How to go from a project or pilot mode to a permanent structure
2. How to get private businesses and other employers on board in the work

In the following, we present the models and discuss considerations and some of the pros and cons that are associated with each of them.

A) The public sector-driven model

In this model, the public sector both initiates the TAM and carries out the operational work. Private companies or e.g. universities looking for talent can use the recruitment and relocation services it provides – which often come free of charge. The model tends to arise from public investment promotion agencies, where the decision to move into the talent area has been a natural one, in order to support investment promotion activities. The private sector can play a legitimising role, by voicing their support for the initiatives and activities carried out.

Figure 3A

Considerations related to this setup:

- The advantage of this model is that there has been a political process resulting in a decision to support a talent attraction initiative. This gives credibility to the initiative and secures initial stable funding.
- However, it can be a slightly fragile setup due to the fact that the employers only play a marginal role. This increases risk of dissatisfaction from the private sector regarding the services delivered – who in consequence might end up developing their own solutions, leading to duplication of work.
- In some instances, scepticism is encountered during the initial phase – however, private businesses tend to change their minds once initiatives begin to display added value. This can lead to the private sector joining in, thereby creating a closer linkage between public and private entities.
- Pilot projects are often financed by either public or EU funds; however, after the initial pilot phase, a more sustainable mix of public and private funding might be reached as a result of the private buy-in.

B) The market- and sponsor-driven model

This model is characterised by a situation where the public sector or Public–Private Partnerships (PPPs) carry out activities and services that are either paid for or sponsored by the business community or employers.

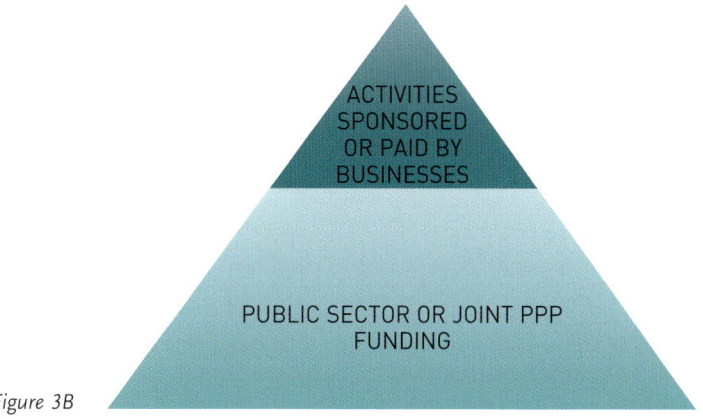

Figure 3B

You may recall the case of Montréal in Chapter Four, where the companies finance international recruitment missions, thereby ensuring their relevance and success.

Considerations related to this setup:

- It requires a high degree of trust between private and public sectors.
- The model has the capacity to deliver more individually-oriented TAM services, catering to the business needs within the region. However, this setup also runs the risk of losing its financial support if requests from businesses should temporarily decrease.
- This model might overlook certain framework conditions due to its reliance on the market, which often acts in a limited spectrum. Examples of frameworks that might be overlooked include urban design, residential planning or improvements of the educational system.
- As we see increased interest from the business community in TAM, there will likely be more examples of the "Market- and sponsor driven model" in the future.

C) *The division of work model*

Opposed to the models we looked at previously, the "division of work model" relies on the idea that the public and private sector take distinctively different roles, complementing each other in the TAM operations carried out. The model can be illustrated by the Singaporean approach, where the public sector plays a strong leadership role with the objective of legitimising and stimulating investments into TAM.

It is worth keeping in mind that this division does not exclude certain basic public sector involvement. In the case of Singapore, this includes public involvement in actively seeking to attract world-class educational institutions to Singapore.[17]

---

17   Campuses or centres of excellence include two types of actors: 1) affiliates to leading universities such as Yale University, Johns Hopkins University, Insead, Massachusetts Institute of Technology (MIT), etc. and 2) a number of leading research and training institutions owned by multinationals, e.g. Sony.

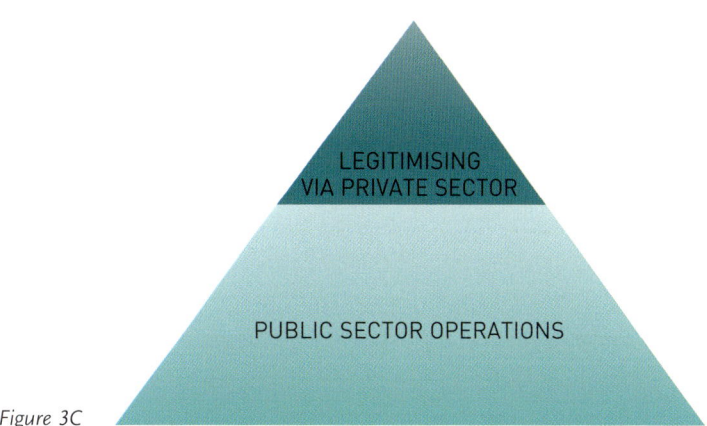

Figure 3C

Considerations related to the "division of work" model:

- Most of the examples of division of work models are found in either Asia or North America; however, many of the lessons learnt from these are transferrable and relevant to a European context.
- Public servants, including mayors and place managers, are often prepared to take a legitimising and leading role. If you are a private sector operation finding yourself in the division of work model, then do not forget to make use of these players to legitimise the activities carried out.
- The model ensures that the business community demands TAM activities at all times, and the strong commercial foundation for the operations promotes innovation and excellence in service design.

D) The network model

The network model adds flexibility to the TAM operations by linking various initiatives between the triple-helix or the so-called "quadruple-helix" actors:

- Business and entrepreneurs
- Academia
- Public bodies and social entrepreneurs
- Other resourceful individuals within civil society

This network approach is open to all sorts of stakeholders – the only requirement is that they have the will and the capacity to contribute to the network. The model is based on the idea that talents coming into a location have different needs, and therefore different entry points. Instead of having a linear chain all attracted talents need to go through, the focus is rather on different points of entry, providing the talent with a welcoming and positive experience, no matter who is in charge. The networking model has an open approach and is characterised by the capacity to expand its resources by involving many different stakeholders. The Copenhagen regional strategy case, outlined in Chapter Two, is to a large extent an illustration of the network approach.

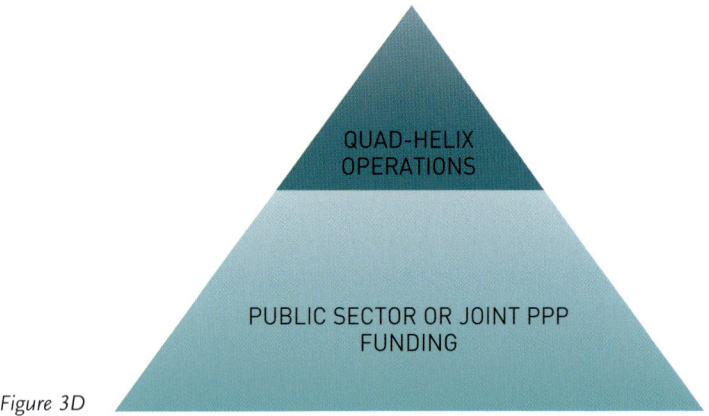

Figure 3D

Considerations related to the "network model":

- The model does not necessarily require the creation of new organisations – or even new projects for that matter – but can instead be based on open coordination.
- In order for this model to work, there needs to be a high degree of trust and at least some degree of established knowledge-sharing, either an informal or formal working relationship, from which to build. It should be considered, however, that the lack of a formal leadership role in the network can reduce the efficiency of activities.

- The underlying nature of TAM, including the attraction of a variety of talent – with different skills, backgrounds and expectations – means that the understanding of individual talent is critical. The network model allows for tailor-made services by mobilising many different stakeholders.

E) The Talent Attraction Arena-centric model

The Talent Attraction Arena (TAA) is defined as "a combination of talent, culture, specialised knowledge and physical place that together form a unique place offering in a certain domain".[18] TAAs are all about creating a talent-oriented place offering, providing soft and hard factors that stand out in a national and international context. They can be geographically concentrated innovative milieus or arenas that attract people sharing the same lifestyle or interests. TAAs often take place in the form of science parks or clusters and the advantage of the model is that it creates a close link between employers and the TAA. The TAA-centric model is all about promoting the arena (be it cluster, science park or any other form) and can help bring credibility and focus – i.e. through place branding campaigns. An example of this is the EnergyVaasa cluster in Finland and its Energy Ambassador Campaign (read more about this example in Chapter Six).

Considerations related to the "Talent Attraction Arena-centric" model:

- Talent Attraction Arenas are dependent on a strong, attractive image of the surrounding city or region. When talents are considering relocating to a TAA, aspects such as the attractiveness of the region and liveability will be relevant to their decision making.
- Choosing this model does not necessarily ensure quality throughout the entire TAM process. However, it does ensure a more focused approach and adds value to talent reputation efforts.

---

18   Tendensor (2014)

Governance and funding models

In order to secure successful management and orchestration of the TAM ecosystem, governance needs to be made a priority. Building a strong governance team comprising partners/individuals from governing parts of the public sector, academic institutions, civil society and corporate management will help ensure that people who have a stake in the area, and who also share insight into the problem, can create a united vision – thereby benefiting the ecosystem holistically. In particular, it is a great idea to consider including the target group of global talent when setting the requirements for the organisation and when developing the ideas for talent attraction and retention services. This can furthermore help you ensure that the talent attraction and retention activities do not become "detached" from the real-world problems and issues faced by talents, but rather deliver solutions that have a real value to the people you are trying to attract.

An interesting illustration is Gothenburg, the second biggest city in Sweden, which in the governance structure of its public–private platform 'Global Talent Gothenburg, West Sweden' has included a 'sounding board' of international talent to make sure that new solutions are refined in dialogue with its target group. Here the TAM activities are planned on a project basis, with each project initially running for a two-year period. In this setup, the steering committee is the governing body and comprises representatives from all the public and private funding parties. The process is managed by a principal project manager and a number of sub-project managers. Recommendations related to engaging talent in other ways can be found in Chapter Four.

Serving as another example is Brainport in Eindhoven, the Netherlands. Here Brainport Development's team works with the talent attraction programme of the Brainport Talent Centre, and comprises five staff members, one working full-time and the rest working part-time on the programme (ranging from 8 to 24 hours a week). Most of the team members have a professional background in either HR and recruitment or sales and marketing.

The governing structure relies on a steering committee, which includes Brainport Development employees (the CEO, Programme Director and Project Leader) and people from six of the 28 member companies. The steering committee decides on crucial, strategic issues for the project on behalf of all the partners.

Funding goes hand-in-hand with the governance model and can come from a mix of sources. It may be publicly funded. It may be co-funded, through public–private funding or the involvement of other stakeholders, usually from the academic sector; this funding can take the form of base funding, membership fees, sponsorships or charges from the TAM entity for individual services (the market-driven model). Or it may rely on EU funding.

Brainport Development also provides an illustration of how different funding models can be applied. For example, in the last few years, it has strived to move away from projects that are purely EU- or publicly funded toward projects that are public/private, or in some cases only privately funded. In their experience, publicly funded projects often do not get an appropriate follow-up. Mostly these projects start with the available funds and not the actual demand. Consequently, long-term support from key stakeholders is lacking. Thus, in Eindhoven, the TAM team is funded by Brainport Development with contributions from the municipalities of the region, as well as 28 member companies and knowledge institutes. One important factor for the success of the programme has been that the member companies are represented on both the strategic level and the operational level, and that these people are actively involved and develop the programme mutually, together with Brainport Development and the Brainport Talent Centre team.

Creating public–private partnerships – how public institutions and private business can work together

Just like in any other healthy relationship, things cannot be one-sided. A local or regional organisation and partnership for talent attraction and retention requires more than just understanding the tasks and finding the right model. A shared insight in the value of attracting talents is needed, as well as trust and common values among the partners involved. A dynamic place leadership among public, private and academic stakeholders will help them to join forces behind a talent attraction strategy.

In a European and Nordic context, the TAM approach is often a public-sector driven model; the comparison with typical North American and Asian approaches can be seen in Figure 3.

Generally speaking, the "European approach" includes various models of delivery, where the public sector is the common denominator, initiating the talent attraction activities. Metaphorically, the public sector remains in the driver's seat. The role of the private sector is not excluded; however, the main driving force behind the TAM activities remains within the public sector. Unfortunately, due to a disrupted link between initiatives carried out by the public and private sector, this approach tends to lead to bottlenecks in its functionalities.

This is in stark contrast to the Singaporean approach, where the drivers are found in the private sector. The public sector maintains an important role, by acting as a legitimising force, i.e. through carrying out branding activities, thereby providing additional credibility to the activities driven by the private sector. This approach helps facilitate a smoother and quicker dissemination of information and ideas between public and private leaders responsible for TAM areas.

A third approach, which is somewhere between the two other approaches, can be seen in the US and Canada. It includes characteristics from both the European and Singaporean approach and relies on a more balanced relationship based on initiatives born in the private sector. There is often a clear allocation of responsibilities, i.e. through joint marketing, where the private sector focuses on direct talent attraction, while the public sector focuses on broader quality of life aspects.[19]

From theory to practice – how change management can help you get started

What is the best way to get started in your work? For new entrants into Talent Attraction Management, we would like to provide two recommendations. The first is to accept an initial phase of experimentation, to make discoveries and learn from shared experiences in the field. These experiences will facilitate the learning process and help you gain more information to make informed choices. The second recommendation is to build on well-functioning, existing structures. This will allow the opportunity to enhance co-coordination between different stakeholders in the TAM eco-

---

19 Tendensor (2014)

system instead of creating new, specialised talent attraction organisations. That said, it is possible that gaps may be identified in the process. If so, new organisations may need to be created. For example, an expat centre might be needed, but is currently lacking. Once this gap is identified, steps can be taken to build such a centre and close the gap.

In some cases, a more comprehensive regional or local change management process is needed to produce the right effects. There may be a need to create a sense of urgency, involve different stakeholders and align their visions and ambitions to agree on a way forward – and in a broader sense, influence the culture of the place and its economic development. As described previously, Talent Attraction Management requires an orchestrated effort from different actors working together in a systemic way. In order to establish such a system, a shared vision is needed, as well as trustful relations and motivated key individuals. Naturally, there could be a gap between the current situation in the region and the desired way of managing talent attraction. A change process can be started to introduce a new way of working.

Nordic Place Academy has developed a framework for managing change in a place setting. It is inspired by Harvard professor John P. Kotter's eight steps of change, which have been adapted to a place setting, and complemented with lessons learnt from managing change processes in a local and regional setting.

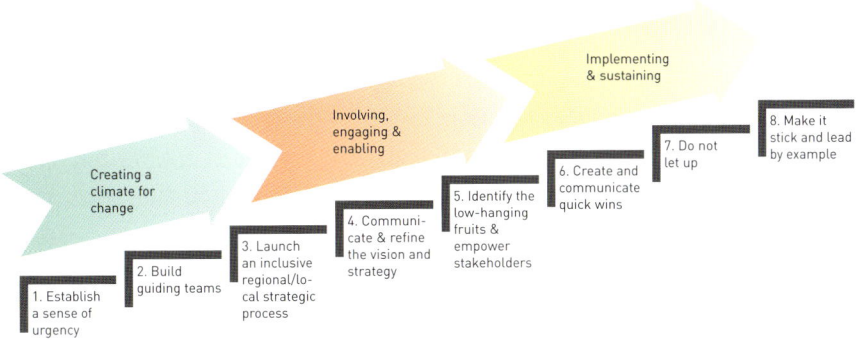

Figure 4: Eight steps of change management in a local or regional setting
Source: Nordic Place Academy (2016), modified from John P. Kotter's eight steps of change

Step 1. Create a sense of urgency around a single big opportunity or crisis

It is critical to create awareness of the need for strategic change. A point to remember is that change does not usually come from fear, but from pointing to a great opportunity. That said, a location that is facing a crisis or looming crisis (e.g. a large number of companies moving out because they cannot find the highly skilled workers they need) may need to use this as a starting point for new opportunities. Instilling a sense of urgency based on addressing the crisis can help pull resources together and force creative and goal-oriented thinking. In addition, benchmarking with frontrunner locations can be a concrete tool for creating a sense of urgency. If your competitors are far ahead, you need to catch up.

Steps 2 & 3. Build guiding teams and launch an inclusive regional/local strategic process to create a vision and strategy

Pooling resources also means connecting people to your change idea and selling the concept in the right way. We suggest you assemble a guiding team with the necessary credibility, skills and connections to provide change leadership – optimally, including the international talent. This team may represent one or several organisations in the location. You should focus on involving key stakeholders in a strategic process to create a sensible, clear, simple and uplifting vision as well as a common strategy.

Step 4. Communicate, seek commitment and refine the vision and strategy

In order to create stakeholder understanding and buy-in, make sure that you communicate the change vision and strategy effectively. This can be done by keeping the communication simple and heartfelt, not complex and technocratic. What will more international talent do for your location? In this step, we recommend using an inclusive approach; this means meeting place stakeholders frequently in order for them to share their input, resulting in refining the strategy based on their interests, and subsequently ensuring their commitment.

Step 5. Identify the low-hanging fruits and empower organisations and people to act on the vision

Identify areas that are easiest to change and begin working with these. Continuously showing success stories encourages and empowers people to further activities and participation. A good example to start with might be sharing positive stories on successful cases of internationals advancing their career thanks to their relocation to your place.

Step 6. Create and communicate short-term wins

Closely linked to step five, remember to communicate results quickly in order to confirm that the efforts are worthwhile. Presenting results can build momentum for next steps. This also helps to legitimise the effort in the eyes of the different stakeholders. Using social media is an efficient tool here, making sure that the improvements and success stories of your initial efforts connect with the involved stakeholders.

Step 7. Never give up

After initial successes, focus on maintaining urgency for long-term results and remove or work around obstacles in the region. An effective way of keeping a sense of urgency is to utilise benchmarking: show how other leading places sustain their efforts. Most talent attraction and retention efforts need time to show long-term results. A simple benchmark example could be Amsterdam. They have spent 11 years and heavy investment in getting the 'I Amsterdam' brand established, which is now showing great results. So do not give up – keep going.

Step 8. Make it stick and lead by example

Keep the change in place by trying to communicate and maintain a new, supportive and strong culture – leading by example is one of the best ways to do this. Here ambassador corps of international talent can play an important role because they will continuously produce new stories of great careers being built. As a result, these stories will communicate and resonate value in the minds of involved stakeholders.

References

Nordic Place Academy (2016). *Handbook on Business Attraction Management for Cities and Regions.* http://placeacademy.com/publications/ September 23, 2016.

Tendensor (2014). *Handbook on Talent Attraction Management for Cities and Regions.* http://tendensor.com/publications/ September 23, 2016.

Interview with Yvonne van Hest, Brainport Development

Yvonne van Hest, Programme director for international labour market development, Brainport Development

Why is it necessary for European cities and regions to work with Talent Attraction Management?

The way I see it, there are a number of important reasons: First of all, we need to fill immediate vacancies; basically all of Western Europe, but also other parts of the world, face critical labour shortages. If you cannot attract the talent your employers need, they might go elsewhere.

We also see that access to talent has become the number one reason for attracting foreign direct investments (FDI) – if you don't have enough talent the investors will go somewhere else, and you will miss out on new jobs.

Finally, there is the innovation argument. If you, as a place, can create a diverse, international community, you will be able to enhance innovation. Diverse teams are more innovative than homogenous teams.

What do you as a place to attract and retain talent?

You need to work with the whole circle and take a holistic view: activities to support attracting talent, settling in, and 'living in' are all dependent upon each other.

You also need to understand your strengths and target group wishes: there is a big difference between Eindhoven and the really big cities. People go to Berlin or London primarily because of the vibrant life, but they come to our region, Brainport, mainly for the jobs, the content of the jobs and their professional development. Even many students who come here do so because of career prospects. Smaller cities need to focus on providing jobs with interesting content.

Also, different target groups have different preferences: IT people may have different wishes from marketers or HR people. At the same time, the 'living in' aspects, such as dual career issues, housing and the presence of international education are also becoming more important for our region.

You are one of the pioneers in Europe in this field – what are the key lessons you have learnt in your work?

Number one is that you have to make sure you understand who your primary stakeholders are: Who am I doing this for, and what do they want? The work will be different depending on whether you are doing it 'only' for your government or if you are also doing it for your companies. If you are doing it for employers, the focus will be more on their shortages and how to fill the open positions they have, at least in the shorter term.

And, in short, if you manage to listen to what your employers want, you are off to a good start. At the same time, you will need to understand the collective will of the companies, because they have different needs.

It is also of great importance to establish trust: the firms, the regional governments and educational institutions all need to trust each other as well as me and my team if we are to collaborate in an effective way.

You also need to stay adaptive and dare to try new things in order to generate new solutions, and to be able to understand what works and what doesn't work.

Last but not least, you have to have the right skills in your team. The team needs to master how to listen to and work with many different stakeholders and marketing professionals, as well as how to work within a political environment – because you need to do a lot of lobbying, policy advocacy and fundraising.

6 Talent Attraction and Place Branding

Places like New York, London, Silicon Valley, and Berlin benefit from their reputations as global magnets for investment, business – and talent. These places have most probably been awarded this reputation because they *are* great places, not primarily because they have branded themselves in a certain way.

And that is the first lesson learned from our collective experience of place branding: the best way to gain a good reputation is to be what you desire to appear, as the ancient Greek philosopher Socrates aptly put it. Marketing communications can play a role in place branding, primarily as a way to augment the positive aspects of the place, but they can never replace the more far-reaching and substantial work of making the place more attractive.

With that caveat in mind, place branding can offer many useful strategies and tools for a place that wishes to attract more talent – just do not expect it to be a quick marketing fix.

In the specific context of this book, the goal for the branding process is to enhance the image of the place in the eyes of talent, and therefore improve the general capacity for attraction of talent. The goal for the marketing process is to package and sell the place, i.e. getting the talent actually to be interested in the place to begin with, and then take the plunge and relocate.

In this chapter, we will discuss different place branding objectives and characteristics of innovative place branding, before finally presenting successful talent attraction marketing strategies.

We do not offer a complete exercise in place branding based on academic theories and the findings of place branding experts; rather we offer our own experiences from the field of place branding and research into talent attraction.

Six branding objectives

We find that there are six main aspects of the brand of a place that can be emphasised when initiating a place branding effort to attract international talent. These are outlined in Table 1.

Table 1: Framework for place branding

Visibility	Being known and recognised
Reputation	Building trust
Differentiation	Standing out from the crowd
Identity	Belonging and identification
Authenticity	Being real
Purpose	Having a role to play in a global world

Source: Modified from Nordic Place Academy, 2016

The first dimension, *visibility*, is about reaching out and getting your voice heard in the noisy, crowded world of place messages. People are reluctant to move to a place they have never heard of. And chances are you are less known "out there" than you think you are or would like to be. In addition, places need to be particularly visible in those focus areas or industries to which they especially want to attract talent. In other words, you need less general noise and more targeted visibility.

Reputation is the overall trust or positive perception talents or other target groups feel for the place. It can be earned by having overall attractive qualities or values in a city, or by performing at high levels in more specific areas, from cultural aspects such as entertainment or sports events to being the leader in a certain industry.

Differentiation is about standing out from the crowd and being noticed as a place. Developing and communicating the unique features of a place is key for differentiation. We argue that innovation will play an increasing role for projecting uniqueness and differentiation. For example, Estonia's dedication to creating an e-society, combined with its disruptive approach of offering e-residency, has created a strong differentiator for the country.

Identity is about the meaning and significance that people living in a place assign to it. It is the flipside of image. Without some level of common identity in a place, there can hardly be an external image. The sustainable development of a place brand needs people who care about it, feel that they belong there and can identify with other residents and the lifestyle of the place. Strategies that enhance the identity of the place can include involving citizens in co-creation of place and local neighbourhoods, as well as in their marketing and communication efforts. Another strategy is to make sure that there is consistency between external messages and local perception of the place, which necessitate that you take steps to understand both its self-image and its external image.

Being *authentic* means being true or real, as opposed to copied, generic, artificial or mass-produced. When Denmark participated in the World Expo 2010 in Shanghai, they displayed the original sculpture the Little Mermaid, which normally sits on a rock in Copenhagen. Few other participating countries in the expo succeeded in connecting to people's cultural interests as Denmark did, resulting in a large number of visitors to the Danish pavilion. Initially, it almost caused an uproar in Denmark, when it was suggested that the national icon could be sent on her first trip abroad in a hundred years. But in the end, and for this particular situation, it was the right thing to do in order to be authentic in telling the story of the Hans Christian Andersen fairytale image of Denmark – a fairytale that resonates particularly well in China.

Brighton in the UK is another example. It has transformed itself from a sleepy tourist town into a hub for young creatives, by leveraging its authentic heritage, culture and attractive lifestyle in combination with the creation and communication of an attractive ecosystem of amenities that cater to this group, such as cafés and restaurants, pedestrian streets, co-working spaces and digital festivals.

We argue that authenticity is a quality that will become increasingly important as the competition between places increases. People want to know the true or real place and what it stands for. The initial implication is that presenting one polished image of the place will not work. Talent will want to see the full picture of the place, both the positive and negative aspects.

When it comes to projecting authenticity, places with a long history may have an upper hand when compared to 'newer' places in, for example, East Asia and the Gulf States. Dubai has many positive qualities, but authenticity may not be the first thing that comes to mind.

In a changing world, projecting a global *purpose* is a smart branding strategy. This resonates quite well with the belief systems of the millennials, who will be increasingly taking over the workforce in the coming years. Places that manage to find a role to play in certain fields where their competences and resources can be combined to give them a natural edge in the market are in a strong position to attract more talent. Estonia's use of its 'e-credentials' to create global purpose and a strong positioning that is hard to copy is a vivid illustration. Lessons from successful places show that a strong place leadership is needed, as well as willingness among the local stakeholders to take risks.

All in all, the more of the six dimensions that can be emphasised in branding the place, the better, but, as outlined, some of them are more powerful than others. Alongside authenticity, a place's purpose also stands out as an effective branding strategy element, in our opinion.

In the next section, we will discuss our four principles of successful and innovative place branding.

Four principles of innovative place branding

Place branding is, as already explained, so much more than marketing. In this section, we put forward four principles of sound and innovative place branding to attract talent.

1. Innovation makes the difference

The competition between places is tough, and it has been increasingly challenging for places to differentiate and convey uniqueness. In such a context, innovation is one of the best ways to stand out from the crowd and get noticed as a place. The most successful efforts worldwide have managed to innovate in making work attractive to talent, and have simultaneously received media attention that you cannot buy – just because they have been so innovative in their approach. The innovativeness of Estonia and Start-Up Chile has created international recognition, as has already been mentioned several times in this book. Another vivid example comes from Oulu in northern Finland, which organises the Polar Bear Pitching event every year – a hole is cut through the ice and entrepreneurs pitch their start-up ideas as long as they can, in the freezing cold. The unique event is broadcasted all over the world and contributes to the image of Oulu as one of the best cities for start-ups in the world. At first glance, it may seem like "just" a marketing stunt, but the event is closely linked to the habits and identity of northern Finland – relating back to the subject of authenticity stressed earlier in this chapter.

2. Co-creation means better solutions, credibility and cost-effectiveness

The best place development, branding and marketing is co-created. Places that manage to harness the creative power that lies in involving talents themselves in place development and place marketing will be the winners of the future. Copenhagen successfully involves international students currently residing in Copenhagen in their marketing efforts towards recruitment of future international students, along with other target markets, as outlined in previous chapters. Vancouver in Canada has opened up its city hall to work with students in projects to make it the greenest city in the world. The results? Talents are attracted to these cities by peer-to-peer recommendations, they stay longer and they become ambassadors of the place. What is more, co-created marketing is more credible and cost-effective than any paid marketing can ever be.

3. It is not (just) about you

As stated above, conveying the purpose of the place and standing out in a heated global competition for attention is one branding objective for places. Many places start with the question of what others can do to contribute to their place, but we argue that you should flip the coin and ask what you as a place can do for others (if a certain John F. Kennedy quotation comes to your mind, you are following our thoughts as well). As mentioned earlier, Estonia introduced an innovative feature in their government services, the e-residency, in 2014. Now anyone in the world can become an e-citizen in an EU Member State and do business with the tools 'E-stonia' provides them with. It is not only a useful tool for people in other countries. It is also a symbolic action with strong communicative power that lends credibility to the highly digitalised and *tech savvy* reputation of E-stonia – and helps to elevate the country's role, position and purpose in the world.

4. Earn a reputation by showing, not telling

We have already mentioned the famous dictum of Socrates, that the best way to create a good reputation is to be what you desire to be seen as. A more modern variation is 'show, don't tell'. The best branding strategies we have seen embody the idea that you become what you want to be as a place. Chile, again, changed its image by becoming an entrepreneurial hub, not primarily by communicating that it was. Manchester in the UK wants to be the 'original modern' city, a reputation that is earned by letting this motto permeate city policies and efforts, for example new cultural activities. This led to the creation of the Manchester International Festival, which in a short period of time has positioned itself as a high-profile cultural event.

Marketing strategies and campaigns in practice

Against the background explained above, what marketing strategies can you use in practice?

The previous sections, together with Chapter Four, have already outlined a number of general success factors for talent attraction, such as the importance of involving both talents and employers in marketing and finding your niche.

With these success factors in mind, let us turn to six campaign types that have proven successful for other regions.

1. Employer-place branding through tools for co-branding and co-marketing

As outlined in Chapter Three, creating a toolbox for employers so that they can tell the story of the place is a successful strategy. Copenhagen and Denmark created an online toolbox where companies can access videos, testimonials, texts, infographics, brochures and photos communicating the culture and qualities associated with life in Denmark.

Such toolboxes can form a starting point for *employer-place branding*, i.e. campaigns that help build the brand both of individual employers and of the place where they are located.

Another viable employer-place branding strategy is to invite employers to use social media channels that are set up by public organisations that have a mandate to promote the place. The "Move to Stockholm" initiative introduced in Chapter Four is a good example of this. You may recall the example of a new tech firm hosting or 'curating' the social media account. Guidelines have been developed in close dialogue with the firms, which encourage the firms to share open positions, insights into their work content and aspects of culture and life in Stockholm.

An important objective of the social media account and other communication activities is to showcase the breadth of the start-up scene. This helps both to attract talent from abroad and to grow the pool in the city.

The thinking goes that people who move to a place want to know that there are other opportunities, should they be dissatisfied with the job they moved for. It is also vital to showcase to those who already live in the city that there are multiple career opportunities available; some people who have been part of a fast-growing start-up that has matured and become a bit 'corporate' may want to join a smaller firm to be part of a rapid growth phase again. Conversely, some people who are currently part of a more nimble company may seek the stability of the more mature, stable firms. The team behind the Twitter account has therefore made efforts to make sure that the weekly hosts of the account are not only the 'usual suspects' but also smaller, less well-known firms.

2. Creative and humoristic campaigns

Innovation is becoming increasingly important to catch people's attention of people, including when it comes to marketing, as claimed at the beginning of this chapter. Using creativeness as well as humour are important aspects of getting attention.

Jönköping in Sweden managed to re-attract talent to the city with a creative, fun campaign. Their campaign was primarily targeted towards talent who already had a link to Jönköping – being a native of the city or having studied there – and, most importantly, who had a personal connection to somebody currently in Jönköping. As a first step, the campaign leaders reached out to people living in Jönköping and asked them to nominate someone that they wanted to move back to the city and who today lived in one of the three biggest cities in the country.

As a result, they identified a gross list of around 300 talents, whom they called "missed people", and through research found out where they lived and worked today. Not only were they contacted directly with an offer to move back, but they would also be confronted with their name displayed on a large billboard ad at the bus or tram stand closest to their home: 'Mr. or Ms. XX [name of talent], please move back to Jönköping, Mr. or Ms. YY [name of person who had nominated them] is waiting for you'. The campaign was an instant success and 22 percent of those targeted actually moved back.

The campaign was supported by several other initiatives, and one in particular gained a lot of publicity: a free online shop with a collection of compelling incentives – of both real and more humoristic value – to facilitate talent relocating to Jönköping, e.g. a settling-in package, a good-bye present for your soon-to-be former boss, assistance in finding accommodation, a free kebab meal on the main street etc. It was all organised and set up as an online shop where the customer (in this case, the requested talent) could select the products and add them to their basket. The ads on the bus stands and the free web shop received a significant amount of media coverage due to the high level of creativity and humour behind them.

Or perhaps you remember the Australian 'Best Job in the World' campaign that ran in 2009? Widely regarded as one of the most successful tourism marketing campaigns ever, Tourism Queensland advertised for the position of 'Island Caretaker' in classified advertisements around the world. The job would require no experience, demand only a single blog post to be written each week, offer free accommodation on one of the islands on the Reef, and pay a six-figure salary. To apply, candidates would need to produce and upload a 60-second video to a website. The campaign became an instant success for Queensland and created much more media coverage than a budget of $1.2 million normally would.[20]

Inspired by Tourism Queensland, the cluster organisation EnergyVaasa in Finland launched a campaign in 2012 called 'Finland's Best Summer Job'. With a projected need to attract up to 10,000 talents to the region's energy technology firms over the coming decade, drastic measures were required to put the region on the map.

The energy ambassador's job consisted of getting to know the Vaasa region and its top energy technology companies by working one week for each company and sharing their experiences mainly on social media. For the three-month job, the ambassador earned a sizeable € 30,000, plus a number of benefits including four-star accommodation, car, occupational

---

20 After only six weeks, more than 34,000 applications had been received from nearly 200 countries. The website drew more than 6.8 million unique monthly visitors with nearly 54 million page views and an astounding average time on site of 8.25 minutes. More than 46,000 mainstream media stories and 230,000 blog posts referred to the promotion, reaching an estimated 3 billion people and earning more than $260 million in media value. Great Britain's BBC would film a documentary about the promotion attracting more than 4 million viewers, and nearly half a million online votes were tallied in selecting the person who would take on the Island Caretaker's role. Source: http://www.sapientnitro.com/content/sapientnitro/en-us.html#work/featured/tourism-queensland/best-job-in-the-world/the-ask/the-ask2.

health care, banking and investment services and daily consumer goods, arranged by the campaign partners.

The campaign has received very positive attention, both before, during and after the summer job. The media visibility and interest was significant and focused on three different phases: the launch, recruitment process and the actual job period. The value of the visibility that was received in the media is estimated at € 3 million (the campaign cost a total of €150,000). On social media results were equally good, with some 100,000 views per week on Facebook, 20,000 views on YouTube and 30,000 views of the ambassador's blog.

The region's businesses are cooperating in the campaign, and the recruitment ads in national print media have borne fruit; the Vaasa region is now known for its energy technology throughout the country. Many employers saw the number of applicants for roles increase remarkably after the campaign. The success of the campaign sparked a repeat in 2013, however, this time the ambassador worked at an international location of one of the companies based in the Vaasa region.

3. *Content and peer-to-peer engagement marketing*

Content marketing is all about creating and distributing valuable, relevant and consistent content to attract and retain a clearly defined audience. *Peer-to-peer marketing* focuses on encouraging your target groups to promote your offering to their peers.

Brainport Eindhoven Region and its development agency Brainport Development is a pioneer when it comes to both content and peer-to-peer marketing. Their latest innovation, TalentBOX (introduced in Chapter Four), is an information and marketing portal and recruitment database that also can be used to mobilise the target audience of talent in the region as well as abroad in content-related engagement. The focus here is the content of the jobs, which is the core focus in the region's attraction efforts, as explained by Yvonne van Hest in the interview just preceding this chapter. The region will never be able to compete with the buzz of cities like London or Berlin, but it can compete to offer career opportunities, interesting high-tech jobs – and edgy content. The region believes that reaching out to peer-to-peer networks with interesting, specific content will become more and more important for talent attraction. When many regions can offer the same type of jobs, the specific content profile of a region can become a key differentiator.

This content-focused engagement is executed in three main ways:

- Stories: Peer subject stories from the tech and IT talents in the companies that will be placed on the talentBOX website (employer pages) and disseminated in special interest groups in diverse social media
- Challenges: Live and online challenges about a specific peer topic from the employers in which worldwide talent can participate
- Webinars and events on relevant content for the target group

One result of this new strategy is that there will be a shift in the region's collaboration with employers, with less focus on working with HR and recruitment functions and more on general management as well as core functions, such as product development, of organisations.

4. Targeted recruitment missions

Recruitment missions that target certain markets and/or groups can be an effective way of attracting talent to a region. Targeting markets that share a language or have a cultural affinity with your place is one possible strategy, as is targeting regions with a known surplus of specific competences.

An interesting illustration of these strategies comes from Montréal in Canada. The flagship service of Montréal International is a series of successful recruitment missions, targeting cities that have close cultural ties with the Québec region and large talent pools within strategic areas compatible with Québec's skills shortage. Montréal International has organised more than 12 recruitment missions and helped approximately 80 companies meet with more than 30,000 professionals. This has led to the hiring of 800 strategic and experienced workers in sectors such as ICT, gaming and aerospace. One important prerequisite for successful recruitment missions is building relationships with local partners in the host destination and informing the government that the mission is taking place, in order avoid friction.

Typically, programme management performs one to three trips to target the market and pave the way for the mission. The participation of professionals on the recruitment missions is by invitation only and for each mission, and approximately 12,000 register. From these, around 2,000 are shortlisted and the Québec firms typically chose between 50 and 250 candidates for actual interviews.

While Montréal targets mainly French- and Spanish-speaking countries where there is a larger pool of talent, Swedish regions have targeted regions in Finland, where many people know Swedish and where there is a large surplus, especially of engineers who have been made redundant after Nokia's hardships and eventual downsizing.

In Scotland, many ICT professionals are from Poland, Portugal and Spain. Scottish Enterprise, in their initiative Digital Talent Scotland, targets these countries by involving people from these countries who are already in Scotland. As ambassadors they will promote Scotland as a career destination both through social media and targeted visits to chosen university recruitment fairs. This also represents a peer-to-peer marketing strategy. In 2016, TalentScotland introduced its first virtual recruitment fair in a partnership with EURES. The online conference, which took place over a whole day, featured company presentations and international talents all sharing their employment opportunities and employee experiences, as well as giving an introduction to relocation aspects. All the online presentations were recorded, offering participants and others an opportunity to go back and revisit the content at a later stage. The online recruitment fair was well attended by the three target markets and is definitely an interesting area to explore in the future for other regions as well.

5. Using open innovation as an attractant

Although not a marketing strategy per se, using open innovation platforms and networks can form quite powerful attraction factors for talent. Their very nature as open arenas that focus on opening up organisations to inter-organisational collaboration makes them well suited for involving students or other talents who are new to a region. They can also enhance social and professional integration of new people, additionally making them important for talent retention.

As mentioned earlier, Vancouver in Canada is working with students in its 'City Studio' program to solve environmental challenges the city faces. The City Studio has become so well-known that many students now choose to study in Vancouver just because they have heard about the programme.

Demola is a university–business cooperation concept originating in Finland but now present across Europe and in Mexico. The idea of the Demola concept is to facilitate concrete projects that test new ideas and mobilise university student talent. Multidisciplinary teams of university students, in collaboration with companies, produce demonstrations of new products, services and social practices, and gain the ownership of IPR that makes entrepreneurship possible. Locations that have a Demola node testify that it has helped them both attract new students to their cities, and retain them after their studies.

6. Digital campaigns

The big advantage of digital campaigns is the flexibility, cost-effectiveness and the possibility of continuing the dialogue with potential candidates. As mentioned in Chapter Three, Denmark has been running digital employer place branding campaigns over the past few years. Together with a number of Danish-based companies within three clusters (IT, cleantech and life science), available positions in Denmark were posted alongside Greater Copenhagen information promoting it as an interesting career destination. The campaigns are based on solid research of where the potential candidates for the open positions are currently located, i.e. in which countries, regions and cities, and where the probability is highest that they will be willing to relocate to Copenhagen. When the right potential candidates are identified, the campaigns try to reach them on the digital platforms where they are active – that is, for example, on websites, e-journals, professional magazines etc. Through articles and web banners with slogans like "Empower your career, think Denmark" or "100 Danish companies are looking for you, what are you looking for?", the campaign tries to direct their attention to the possibilities on offer in Denmark. If the international talent becomes curious, they can, through a single click, be redirected to the campaign platform with all the open jobs available and easily go on to the career sites of the companies taking part in the campaigns. Likewise, they can find a lot of information on the industry sector and what it is like settling in as an international in Denmark.

Over the past year, an even more targeted form of digital campaign has been developed. From attracting a variety of different jobs for many companies within a broad industry sector like ICT, a few companies within a more segmented sub-industry like gaming are now joining forces and collaborating to attract specific profiles, e.g. back-end programmers or game developers. This allows the campaign to be even more targeted by adding the possibility for the interested candidates to register and receive more information on upcoming job offers. Simultaneously, a talent pool is being built for long-term coverage of the skills gap within the gaming industry.

References:

Nordic Place Academy (2016). *Handbook on Business Attraction Management for Cities and Regions.* http://placeacademy.com/publications/ September 23, 2016.

Interview with HRH Prince Joachim, Danish Monarchy

How would your Royal Highness describe your encounters with international talent in Denmark through the Youth Goodwill Ambassador programme?

On several occasions, I have felt that these young people – representing 50 countries and different cultures – all ooze with energy and express interest in the globalised world. Yet they chose Denmark, even though it is known for its bad and cold weather. That is why these people are so interesting; they carry a different mind-set that challenges the perspective you have on society. I value that highly.

In your experience, how can these individuals act as youth ambassadors and bridge connections between Denmark and their home countries?

Once they settle here as students, they see what Denmark has to offer. Some will stay and continue their studies for longer than planned, some will go abroad and eventually some will be employed in Danish companies. They can add a lot of value to these companies and to their native countries, because they have learned a lot from their stay in Denmark. Wherever they go, there will always remain an anchor in Denmark – a sense of belonging here, which I am sure will create new business opportunities in the long run.

Everybody is an individual and beauty is in the eye of the beholder. Because they arrived with a different culture, they are already contributing towards creating a bridge between their home country and Denmark. When they return to their own culture, their understanding of Danish culture will have become part of their new mind-set. They will have the Danish flavour in their new way of life.

Please elaborate on different mind-sets and how they can become assets.

In the globalised world, your mind-set has to change. For a long period, there was a tendency that Danish universities were content to remain as local-orientated universities. About 10 to 15 years ago it was apparent that they needed to broaden their horizons; they needed to attract more international resources and students. This also adds to the edge and recognition of the university – the more international you are, the more attractive you become. You cannot evaluate that asset in financial terms, but you need to be willing to pursue that trajectory. That is precisely what Danish universities have been doing over the past couple of decades.

Why do you think that the idea of a Youth Goodwill Ambassador Corps is a successful method?

The idea of a youth goodwill corps came from another corps, the Copenhagen Goodwill Ambassador Corps. This corps was formed as a network of influential Danes living abroad with very close ties to Denmark. They work to create relations and business opportunities around the world, on a voluntary basis. Some bright minds in that corps thought: why not do the same with international students in Denmark? That was the foundation of the YGA corps. Today, the YGA programme is also a career programme, assisting the international students taking a full degree in starting and empowering their careers in Denmark. So everybody gains from the programme; it is a win–win and that is why the method works, in my opinion.

You have studied and worked abroad yourself and have a truly international family. What value has this international way of life given you as an individual?

You have to reflect on your own values, you cannot take them for granted. When you are in an international setting, you have to ask yourself what is the positive side to the values you have and what is the negative? That is of tremendous value. It keeps your development going and it allows you to contribute when you are abroad. But you have to be open-minded – if you go into an international setting and you are not open-minded then you cannot absorb all the values. You have to dive in and be a part of it while adding your own flavour to the context.

How can Denmark become more attractive to internationals?

It is interesting to observe how Denmark has become more and more international. This goes on any level, whether it is more international-orientated universities or increased tourism. When I graduated 30 years ago, there were very few international students. That has changed significantly. All that adds to the international flavour of the big cities of Denmark, where people are expecting it and benefiting from it. Thus Copenhagen, Aalborg, Aarhus and Odense have in recent years become more international cities. This in itself makes a country more attractive to internationals, but you need to work on many levels at the same time to make a country even more attractive. Everything from tax to the general environment and international schools is important.

7 Attracting Entrepreneurial Talent

Every seasoned talent attraction manager will recognise that entrepreneurial talent attraction and retention takes the task to yet another level. As much as many activities within talent attraction and retention are pivotal to entrepreneurial support, there are other aspects that need to be accommodated. Firstly, entrepreneurial talent activities require an entire ecosystem of support to function well and enable growth – from first-stage financing, incubators to accelerators, VCs and viable exit opportunities for start-ups. Secondly, infrastructure with institutional support such as legal and accounting advisers, and access to venture-friendly markets, need to be provided. Lastly, an entrepreneurial culture needs to be fostered, comprising both societal norms and access to success stories inspiring the next generation of entrepreneurs.

We will not claim that providing such a comprehensive offer is an easy thing to do. Many cities and regions struggle to appropriately support their native entrepreneurs, enable major growth opportunities, or better yet, attract new start-ups. Having said that, Talent Attraction Management activities can also play an integral role in attracting start-up talent.

Hence, in this chapter we will address the question of what cities and regions do to attract founders and start-ups, even with their limited initial resources, and help them grow in the region.

In our research, we have encountered a few particularly interesting strategies aimed at entrepreneurial talent attraction in locations such as Chile, Tel Aviv, Toronto and Stockholm. These form the basis for our recommendations on how you can create or capitalise on the existing entrepreneurial opportunities in your region.

Entrepreneurial reality

First things first, let us look at why entrepreneurship creates so much hype today and why TAM organisations should engage in supporting it. Entrepreneurial success stories encourage people to dream big and reach for success. Entrepreneurship contributes to the innovation capacity of a place and can boost economic growth significantly, since the biggest job creators in many countries today are fast-growing start-ups. It can be an inspiration to talents stuck in corporate careers or young people still deciding what career path to follow. Entrepreneurial success stories benefit entire communities, also contributing to great place branding.

The barriers of entry to entrepreneurship are becoming lower due to access to technology, and costs connected to testing an idea or setting up a company are decreasing. The fact that some of today's most successful start-up companies base their businesses solely on online activity means that they are in a position to move wherever and whenever it suits them best.

This flexibility propels the competition between cities and regions, allowing them to offer more than the basic TAM support: for example, a vibrant start-up community and access to other successful entrepreneurs, mentors or talents to help new companies reach their growth potential. Still, many start-ups fail to scale-up successfully; that is an inherent part of the business, so to speak. Technology and solution development takes time, especially when today's start-ups often provide really innovative and ground-breaking solutions. In our experience, lack of access to technical or management talent often hinders the transition from start-up to scale-up. This in turn makes talent attraction management extremely important as it can serve as a catalyst for regional economic growth within a successful entrepreneurship environment.

In an entrepreneurial world failing is not necessarily perceived pejoratively, but instead as an opportunity to come up with a better idea. The crucial aspect in terms of the public sector's role, however, is that the right kind of support must be provided by the local ecosystem and that the entrepreneurs who succeed and fail are enabled to use their expertise in other ventures. The best-case scenario resulting from a well-functioning ecosystem is when the local entrepreneurs who have gone through a large exit or IPO want to return and give back to the community, often becoming angel investors themselves. It is all about seeing the bigger picture, as any of the steps could lead to a spill-over effect – something that any city or public representative would surely appreciate. Here, Talent Attraction Management can play an important role in facilitating mobility of talent, so that those with ideas and experience can be of help to start-ups that are ready to grow. In the next section, we will outline practical recommendations for Talent Attraction Management in the start-up context.

Tools and recommendations for entrepreneurial talent attraction

At this stage it needs to be highlighted that start-ups also need talent, making a well-functioning TAM support structure in a location important.

Just like any other company in a growth phase, start-ups need talent and want to tap into places that can offer the talent they require. Successful entrepreneurs think big, on a global scale, and thus moving to where the resource is located does not necessarily pose a challenge. Some of the forerunners in entrepreneurial ecosystems deploy measures to address this and meet the demand of the mobile world. But attracting entrepreneurial talent is not only about meeting the recruitment needs of current start-ups; it is also about getting those that are potential founders of new firms to consider your city or region.

Tel Aviv is known for its strong entrepreneurial capacity, as well as its abundance of engineers and tech talent emerging from the local universities and even the Israeli military. Access to the best technology and the experience gathered during their military service equips local talent with problem-solving skills and a determination to provide new solutions to real-life problems. This creates a knowledge hub that attracts international corporations to set up their R&D centres there, multiplying the innovation capacity of Tel Aviv and leading to a self-reinforcing effect.

When it comes to entrepreneurs who enter the scaling-up stage, however, the diversified skills needed are not often found locally. Furthermore, access to mentors, and also appropriate funding, is not always available in Tel Aviv.

So how are these challenges addressed? Firstly, the entrepreneurial attitude and conducive culture is strongly supported in Tel Aviv. Interestingly, the city consciously works to develop its own brand, separate from that of Israel; it specifically promotes itself as entrepreneur-friendly. Secondly, the limited size of the domestic market pushes local people to search for opportunities abroad. Thirdly, due to many successful entrepreneurs coming from Tel Aviv and Israel, the network one can reach out to is widespread and relatively easily accessible.

All this combined leads to a situation where many start-ups venture out to other markets (e.g. Silicon Valley), to set up second offices and tap into the resources there, while keeping the head offices in Tel Aviv and ensuring local talent flow.

Another initiative Tel Aviv introduced to attract entrepreneurs and enable their development is the Innovation Residency Program, which was set up to enable international entrepreneurs to move to Tel Aviv for a limited period and experience the ecosystem at first hand. Dozens of cities are offered this opportunity to collaborate and invite entrepreneurs to their ecosystems; however, any entrepreneur is welcome to apply on his/her own as these city agreements are non-binding.

In similar fashion, Berlin is building strategic alliances with top-ranking ecosystems to promote exchange, cooperation and sharing of talent. The most recent initiatives include a pilot programme with New York, as well as participation in the Innovation Residency Programme introduced above.

Promote a positive image of entrepreneurship

The need to promote a positive image of entrepreneurship and the conducive culture to grow the talent pool cannot be stressed enough. One needs to create an environment in which it is easy for business people and researchers to start companies, or go from a secure corporate job to an insecure start-up job, and one needs to create attractive meeting places where people want to spend time working on their projects. Promoting these aspects should be a key task of the city's or region's development organisations.

The entrepreneurial spirit of a place often develops organically, but creating it through a disruptive approach like in the case of Chile is also possible. If developed organically, there are multiple enabling factors and a positive attitude towards entrepreneurship is surely the place to start. Young entrepreneurs often seek to be part of a community with like-minded people and perceive starting a business as a real opportunity career-wise. Strong public sector support for entrepreneurship sends important signals of the importance of entrepreneurship that will help promote a conducive culture. What is more, success stories and other news need to be continuously communicated. The following are "best practice" examples of how a positive image of entrepreneurship can be fostered.

Stockholm Business Region Development has collaborated with the main local English newspaper, as well as more specialised start-up media, in elaborating and publishing editorial content about the start-up scene in the city. It is also supporting or co-organising a range of co-working spaces and events that enable network-building and promote the start-up scene to a wider audience.

In Toronto, the political leadership, including the mayor, often emphasises the importance of promoting the start-up ecosystem. This supportive approach represented by high-level figures and recognition of the economic value created by start-ups and small businesses are important aspects of positive image construction.

Tel Aviv and Israel claim that entrepreneurial drive is in the DNA of their people. Consequently, entrepreneurial ventures are supported across the city and country. Tel Aviv entrepreneurs perceive business failure as a positive step towards a better solution. Therefore, most start-up founders in Tel Aviv are serial entrepreneurs.

Chile's entrepreneurial ecosystem is still very much in the making, but already, local media is taking note of the interesting stories from within the entrepreneurial world. This was certainly not the case in the past.

In summary, keep in mind that a creative and innovative approach to entrepreneurship promotion can take you far.

Start-up communities and co-working spaces

One of the major attraction factors for entrepreneurs is access to a community with attractive meeting places, such as co-working spaces and start-up hubs, where people want to spend time. The attractiveness of the physical space is one important factor, and promoting a community feeling and 'cool vibe' is also key. In addition, rents need to be affordable. As real estate prices increase, regions will need to find ways to offer cool, central and inexpensive locations to start-up hubs, as they want to be in the heart of things, blending work and urban life into one.

Cities like Toronto and Stockholm have understood the importance of these factors and the start-up lifecycle, thus involving various stakeholders in creation of these places. Today in Stockholm, co-working spaces almost automatically attract the start-ups and different essential service providers that help constitute an ecosystem (such as investors, HR consultants and recruiters, legal support, incubator services, etc.). While affordable housing is a challenge in Stockholm, local start-ups are now in a position to speak up about the situation, and if the city wants to keep its entrepreneurial hub, they will need to listen to these start-ups and seek possible solutions.

Berlin serves as another example, as it directly acknowledges that history has paved the way for affordable housing, which is being used for co-working spaces in the centre of the city. Areas of Berlin are now re-emerging with the new life and breath of the entrepreneurial spirit; old, unused buildings are being transformed into exciting areas – gentrification in the making.

These places will help increase the talent pool by contributing to making entrepreneurship more attractive, and by creating new interfaces and networks between people in the ecosystem. Investors and multinational corporations with R&D centres will be attracted to these places, as they represent the heart of entrepreneurship in the city, i.e. an innovation hub as a resource.

Entrepreneurship education and the long-term approach

A strong entrepreneurial environment is mostly constituted by a combination of international and domestic talent. Generally, to create an environment only based on internationals will be difficult. Therefore, you will need to support the development of local talent within entrepreneurship alongside attracting entrepreneurs from abroad. To match the future needs of the talent supply, educating the community and supporting innovative thinking and the entrepreneurial mind-set is necessary. Change is possible, but coordinated efforts and a long-term vision are needed.

The Ministry of Education in Toronto, Ontario, takes a long-term approach in working closely with the educational institutions in the region (universities and colleges, as well as primary and secondary education) to help modernise the education system and promote creativity and entrepreneurship as career opportunities. Furthermore, the Ontario region prioritises funding for university start-ups.

In Stockholm, the Stockholm School of Entrepreneurship offers entrepreneurship education to all main higher education instructions, meaning that future engineers, business graduates, bioscience professionals and art students all share a classroom.

In Finland, many universities are engaged in entrepreneurial activities and particularly Aalto University, which has a Small Business Centre that promotes entrepreneurial education and offers courses in subjects such as the start-up, development and expansion phases of businesses.

In Chile, where the community traditionally has been risk-averse, there has been no available courses for the entrepreneurial individual. Today, less than six years into Start Up Chile, the top five universities have introduced entrepreneurship programmes.

Differentiate and find your talent niche

Sometimes places try to build constructed place brands – as opposed to more organically developed place brands – with a hope of making it attractive to the wider public. However, as seen in many of the successful places used as examples in this book, authenticity is the game changer – even if this does not always mean following the most popular approach. In the competition for talent, some of the TAM practitioners probably realise that the fight is often for the same talent. As obvious as it is due to the current market and demographic challenges, there are still opportunities to specialise and attract the talent that has not been appropriately addressed yet.

As repeated throughout this book, mixing your unique selling points with disruptiveness, business and talent attraction management and then branding it, is the way to go. The Polar Bear Pitching event introduced in Chapter Three is one such example. A result of collaboration between BusinessOulu, university students and entrepreneurs, the event embraces the real Finnish way of life and by taking this bold approach, it instantly attracted entrepreneurs, investors and international media.

Concerning other differentiation possibilities, targeting a specific talent niche could be a real opportunity to build expertise and ultimately an attractive ecosystem. Chile, as an example, has introduced an incubation and acceleration programme targeted at female entrepreneurs. Since women are generally underrepresented in the entrepreneurial community, this approach is a very smart example of how to position your location on the global map. And speaking of authenticity, it just so happens Chile was the first Latin American country to have a female elected president.

Another approach would be to define what your existing ecosystem strengths are, even if they are not in line with the general growth strategy. If you do arrive at a niche sector or area, give it the priority the ecosystem needs to develop a centre of excellence, which can drive the sector towards success.

Similarly, yet in different ways, both Berlin and Austin have listened to the creative vibe that was present in their regions. Berlin created one of the best performing sectors for its economy through the creative industries and Austin built an internationally recognisable brand out of its South by Southwest (SXSW) festival.

Leverage the international community

There is vast potential in working with the international professionals and students who are already in the region, but due to visa regulations struggle to find opportunities to stay beyond the completion of their degrees or make the transition to self-employment.

In most cases referred to in this book, the international community already exists; some cities have been better at harvesting the creative potential and networks of those talented individuals.

Our general recommendation is to include them in the process of improving your ecosystem, empower them to come up with innovative ideas (like the Polar Bear Pitching idea) and utilise their network potential. Most importantly, make sure the infrastructure is there for them to come to, stay in and grow your ecosystem.

Interview with Manas Mani, Nordea

Head of business process excellence, Nordea

How does someone from India end up in Denmark?

As I see it, it is all about grabbing the opportunities that present themselves. I was looking for different MSc opportunities around the world and luckily I stumbled upon an opening in Denmark, which is why I applied for an MSc scholarship through the Erasmus Mundus Mobility for Life programme. At the time, there were only two or three people who got scholarships and I was the only one selected for a full master's programme. And so I headed to Aalborg University for a degree in Innovative Communication Technologies and Entrepreneurship.

When you were looking to study abroad, what factors did you take into account in making your final choice?

I put a lot of effort into actually getting the scholarship. Secondly, it was the subject that I found interesting and relevant to my interests, and I had been in touch with professors and universities in order to request information about various courses. These factors combined assured me that I was on the right path.

Furthermore, I like to explore and travelling around the world became a possibility. Through this, I basically received a full career package, which is why I chose it.

Post degree – what criteria did you consider related to where you wanted to work?

Banking is one of the most important sectors in the economy. It facilitates the efficient flow of credit towards productive activities and contributes to nation-building. It is one of the areas of focus identified by the current government, owing to the importance of the sector driving economic growth. I am very optimistic about the growth of this sector; hence I became part of the process of nation-building through financial inclusion. Also, I wanted to get into the centre of a capital city and I have always found that the banking area is in the core of society. It is a good foundation for seeing the growth around the world and I think banking as a platform allows you to get connected with a lot of different actors. When I finished my studies I had other opportunities as well, but I found banking more interesting, as it is easier for me to serve the world and create a better future for more people through this industry.

How important do you find the place is, in comparison to the specific university or employer that you have pursued in your career?

I like Denmark, as I have experienced a very good work–life balance here. The work culture is great, and there is room for my personal life. Overall, I consider the European work culture to be good, but Denmark is exceptional due to its management practices and the work–life balance. I see this in Nordea, where it is about having good ethics and a strong, transparent and respectful internal culture.

If a region wanted to make itself attractive to you for your future career, how should it promote itself?

It should start with positive and welcoming news in the media. Lately it has mainly been negative, looking through last year's poll results. Change comes from within, and if a country is looking to globalise, it should be reflected in the broad picture. Has it been reflected, what foreigners bring to the country? Are the right strategies in place in order to bring in skilled internationals? Is the government putting enough effort into promoting itself? Is the country welcoming? Digital and social media are representing countries abroad, and negativity through this channel can repel potential skilled international citizens. Individuals see that far-right parties are gaining more popularity, and even tougher citizenship requirements are imposed. This would form a bad image of a country, hence depleting a globalised and international scene, and the attraction of talents.

I am not being negative here; I just don't think that everyone is aware of what is actually happening. I believe that the media should present the advantages of globalisation and of having international talents. The nation has to brand itself and make policies very clear. It needs to address certain questions and be able to answer clearly the question of whether it wants to attract and retain foreign skills. According to some research the Green Card scheme has been repealed, but has any replacement been introduced or considered instead of just closing this programme? Thus, I think Denmark currently lacks an overall strategy in terms of talent attraction.

What can we do to improve – and bring the best talent to Denmark and Europe?

Make sure to publish success stories and the value that internationals bring to this country. Spread the right statistics and good news across local and international media. To secure a better branding, opportunities in the country should be highlighted through either digital or social media around the world. Additional things to consider are easy access to the job market and education, as well as a faster and more effective way of getting a work permit and visa. Online language and cultural training prior to entering the country could also be beneficial for the nation and individuals.

8 On the future of talent attraction – is more innovation needed?

We promised you a practitioner's guide to talent attraction. For those of you who have read from the beginning or jumped around in some of the previous chapters, we hope you have found our considerations useful and that you can use them as inspirations for your own endeavour. For those of you who skipped ahead to this chapter, we welcome you and hope you enjoy reading it.

Our aim in this chapter is to summarise and look ahead. In our own work in trying to innovate talent attraction, several important questions have come to our minds. What will the future bring for those of us who spend many hours making our places attractive for the world's brightest minds? Why on earth are we still moving people around in the digital age? Could we not just use the new ICT tools for working together at a distance? In other words, will there still be a job to do in talent attraction?

We think there will, but our prognosis is that it will change in the years moving forward – both in focus and in content. The issue of attracting international talent has been somewhat separated from the issue of developing local talent. Likewise, talent attraction today is mostly carried out at the national level. We believe that the focus on both issues will change over the coming years; most likely we will witness a merger of the attempts to attract more talent and develop them domestically. Additionally, the locus for attracting will move from the national level to the regional/city level. Furthermore, even though we consider that the 'war for talent' is far from over, more cooperation between regions and cities will appear. Highly skilled people are often opportunity-driven and curious; they will move around to empower their careers and lives. You should be happy and not sad if they choose to spend three to five years of their lives at your location, but then move on to something else. Those years are more than enough to pay back your effort of attracting them. As mentioned earlier, make sure they leave happy and new business opportunities and talent will flow your way. Therefore, the coming decade might be the age of 'collaboration for talent'. Our beautiful world has enough wars to handle.

Innovation – is it just a popular buzzword? It might be that the innovation part of 'innovating talent attraction' will be called something else, but it will not be needed any less. More and more regions and cities realise that one of their main challenges is that they lack talent, especially rural regions, which have been struggling more in recent years. Urbanisation and the lifestyle the metropolises offer is a strong pull factor for bright minds. That is why many new cities are entering the game for their share of talent. Again, common knowledge here, but if you enter a game with well-positioned players already present, you had better come up with something new. To paraphrase Groucho Marx's famous opinion on sex, but with our own personal twist, 'Innovation is here to stay'.

As for the future, how can you trust that we can predict it better than you can? Well, we cannot – and there is an important point hidden here, as we have underlined in the previous chapters. Your work needs to be developed in your context, facing the challenges that your place encounters, and organised in a way that suits you, and the context and the stakeholders you have. Your future might look different from ours but we believe that we all need to make the same considerations and be structured in our way of working. That is why we have delivered a framework for conducting innovative talent attraction – and why you will find a self-assessment tool in the appendix. Both can be good starting points for developing your work with talent attraction. Piet Hein – a Danish poet – once said: 'It is difficult to predict – especially the future'. Our best advice is to take the next step and complement prediction with building your own future. You already live in the most wonderful location; go share it with others!

Will talent attraction still be high on the agenda in the coming years?

The easy answer to the question above is yes. Earlier in this book, we argued that talent attraction will become even more important in the future. Nevertheless, there are good reasons to question why this would be the case. Why move people around the globe in the digital age when there are ICT tools available that allow them to work together at distance? And with more and more companies being truly global in their organisational set-up, you would think that they would be able to attract the skilled talent they need at their different locations.

Beyond a doubt, progress has been made in recent years in developing methods and new divisions of labour for working together across distances and countries. Systems for virtual meetings and knowledge-sharing, e.g. common project management systems for people located in different places, have been around for a while. Many companies are exploring how to take these methods to a new level, changing their organisational structures and thereby creating truly international teams – not by placing people in the same physical location, but rather through departments comprised of members across several countries.

Many sales and project managers are responsible for regions and/or several countries, which they need to visit on a regular basis. Their jobs are not bound to a specific place, meaning that it does not necessarily make sense to have them relocate to another country for a new role, moving their families and so on, if the sales manager is away from home most of the time anyway. Instead, different commuting arrangements can be made. For example, the manager can fly to HQ on Monday for a couple of days, then fly out to sales meetings in various other locations mid-week before flying back home on Friday.

Likewise, new business models are being tried out with different mixes of off-shoring and out-sourcing arrangements. International consulting firms within engineering, recruiting and ICT for many years now have had supporting and calculating subsidiaries in other countries, e.g. India or Ukraine. As a result, these companies gained access to local competences at a lower cost than by requiring people to move around. This takes place not only within companies but also among different cooperation set-ups between companies, that is, having preferred partners with specific competences available in different countries. Some consultancy firms even offer to set up and run specific tasks for other companies in another country. An example here could be some of the global ICT companies who have located their European head offices in Ireland but need people with language skills to cover the support function for all the different languages. Until recently, they have tried to attract people to Ireland to cover the multinational support functions from the same location near Dublin. Increasingly, it is becoming difficult to attract enough people with the right ICT and language skills to relocate. Instead, an external consultancy firm has taken over the task of setting up the support team, and in this particular case it was established in Spain. On behalf of the global ICT company, they will recruit people in Spain and run the support team on a consultancy basis.

These new business models have the potential to reduce the number of people who need to be moved around and attracted to new places. With that said, our prognosis is that these models will not reverse the overall trend. The reasons for a continuous increase in the mobile global workforce are stronger. As we have mentioned some of the reasons previously, we will outline them here again for quick reference:

- *The close connection between talent attraction and foreign direct investments.* If the right skilled people are not present, then the companies will move somewhere else. This means that cities and regions will be eager to attract the most talented people to their location in order to be able to attract international companies.
- *The share of knowledge-intensive tasks is increasing.* These tasks demand a close cooperation between the involved individuals on a daily basis, which is difficult to obtain at a distance. In spite of the development of new ICT tools for collaborating virtually, they cannot compete with the close cooperation you can obtain by being physically present.
- *Corporate values and ways of working need to be learned from within.* Most companies would like their personnel to know and behave in accordance with their corporate values. Therefore, a Chinese manager – who is to take over a department in China for a multinational company– will likely be relocated to HQ for a number of years before letting him/her take over. This is to make sure that the department in China acts in accordance with the values and procedures of the company.
- *The internationalisation of universities.* More and more universities around the world offer international programmes, attracting students from other countries. A proportion of them will commence their careers in the university's surroundings, while more international study programmes will be a driver for talent mobility.

- *Demography and fluctuations in economic growth rates around the world.* As outlined previously, the most important factor is that many countries have a significant need for talent due to demography. The shortage of professionals with the right competences will be a driver for talent mobility. Likewise, the fluctuations in the growth patterns will be an incentive for talent to move around.

From the 'war for talent' to talent mobility collaboration

We have argued that talent attraction will be an important part of the agenda for the coming decades. The regions and cities showing growth are mostly likely to be the ones with a high proportion of international talent. However, bright minds move about and do not necessarily want to stay in the same location for their entire career. Actually, you should not expect them to, or even hope for it. We will all gain from more talent mobility.

Why is talent mobility important? It helps ensure that talents find their way to where they are most needed, have the greatest opportunities and are most productive. Looking at Spain as a recent example, we can take away a couple of relevant insights. In just a couple of years, Spain has gone from being a country of labour immigration to a country of labour emigration. Leading up to the years of financial crisis, lots of talent from Eastern and to some extent northern Europe went to Spain to work, but the tide turned around 2011-2012[21] to a situation where young people from Spain increasingly went abroad to find work opportunities in Germany and UK – two prime recipient countries of the Spanish labour force. As the crisis had created mass unemployment – especially among the younger generation – a well-functioning talent mobility collaboration will help tackle economic crises by providing opportunities for people elsewhere. Conversely, countries that experience talent shortages, such as Germany, will also benefit from the increased mobility. And Spain will – we argue – gain in the long term, if it can successfully leverage the

---

21 In 2012, migration inflows fell to 0.8 percent of the domestic population, from an average of 1.2 percent per year in the period 2008-2010, and outflows rose to 1.2 percent of the domestic population, up from 0.4 percent per year in 2008-2010. Source: Izquierdo et. al. (2015)

skills and competences their diaspora population gains when a proportion of these migrants relocate back to Spain. Meanwhile, the burden of unemployment benefits is lessened for the government. In short, it is a win–win for everyone.

The 1990s expression 'war for talent' mentioned in Chapter One and coined by the McKinsey study is still relevant today, in the ever-increasing competition on a global scale. However, we suggest an alternative solution to a regional talent war. The notion that talent mobility is essential for countries and regions – in both good and bad economic times – forms a rationale for increased cooperation between countries within the talent mobility field. For example, if all cities and regions in Europe became better at building their reputation for attracting, welcoming and integrating talent, while at the same time increasing collaboration in facilitating talent mobility across regions, the conditions for mobility between European countries could increase substantially.

From a European perspective, this is a very important aspect. The European single market rests on the idea of free movement of people, and labour mobility is a critical component alongside the three other 'freedoms' – of capital, goods and services.

It is a known fact that Europe is suffering from much lower mobility than the United States. The differences are striking: research has shown that mobility between EU countries applied to 0.14 percent of the working age population, whereas mobility between states in the US applied to 1.98 percent of the working age population.[22]

In addition, the political climate can be more or less favourable towards international labour mobility and migration depending on the political focus of the governing party or parties. In recent years, we as authors find that in Europe there has been a tendency towards more domestic protection than open borders, making it more important than ever for regions in need of international talent to work actively to ensure talent mobility.

---

22 European Union Regional Policy (2008)

Merging the agendas of domestic and international talent

"Talent is talent and the companies are colour-blind", as one company manager in a born global company put it. Companies just want to attract the necessary talent needed for developing their business. Whether the talent is from the same country as the company or from abroad is becoming increasingly less relevant – what matters is that they can do the job. Historically, many companies first searched the local market for the talent they were looking for, and only if they could not find enough to cover their skills gaps did they go abroad to find highly skilled people from other countries. Likewise, many SMEs were hesitant to recruit international professionals because of language challenges or concerns about whether they could fit into the culture of the existing workforce. This is changing for several reasons.

The globalisation of doing business is one important factor. The expansion of more markets means that what was once a domestic competition has now turned global. You need to have the skills on board to enter new markets abroad. Therefore, companies need to diversify their recruitment in order to find talent with international experience that is capable of doing business internationally. Another sign of this globalisation process is that more companies are changing their corporate language from their national language to English. This not only allows all procedures to be streamlined across countries, but also makes it easier for internationals to enter the company. On top of that, more companies are born global, meaning that they aim for the world market right from the beginning (e.g. ICT start-ups) and often commence with a truly international team from day one (e.g. companies like Tesla and UBER with internationals among the founding members of the company). The reluctance that many companies originally had in getting internationals on board due to language or cultural concerns start to diminish when positions in the company cannot be closed domestically, for instance in core engineering or programming. A smart company might forget about their previous concerns and recruit an international professional, rather than miss business opportunities.

The consequence of this development is that the discussion on international versus national talent is changing. In some places, the focus has increasingly been on attracting international talent, whereas in others, the national talent has been the primary focus. We tend to see a difference between capitals and bigger cities focusing on recruiting more international talent compared to smaller cities and regions, which have concentrated on re-attracting talent originally lost to those larger cities, often for educational and job purposes. But the difference is diminishing more and more. The separation of the issue concerning international and national talent will increasingly be a false one.

Increasing the international experience of the local talent is an important issue in many countries. This can be done through 'internationalisation at home', for instance ensuring study programmes are conducted with international groups while also inspiring the local talent to go abroad to obtain international experiences themselves. The cooperation between Montréal in Canada and the French Government is a good example of this kind of approach; the French government has engaged with the city of Montréal to allow for more French nationals to go to Montréal to work, in spite of the fact that this will lead to a shortage of talent in France. The reason for this is basically that the French government wants more French nationals to obtain international experiences and create bonds to foreign markets, to continue to keep France in a competitive place.

Cities and regions are the new locus for talent attraction

There is a tendency that the key locus for talent attraction is changing from the national level to the level of regions and cities. Before – as a talent – you would be heading for your new job abroad in Canada, whereas now you would be relocating to Toronto or Montréal. This might of course just be a way of speaking, but we think there is more to it than that. The Germany booth at the MIT European Career Fair does not put Germany at the forefront any more, but is replacing it with signs for Berlin and Munich. The universities looking to attract first-class engineers are branding themselves more prominently now than just a few years ago.

A further indication of this tendency is the Global Talent Competitiveness Index. If you look at the list of the top 10 frontrunners of the index over the first three years the study has been conducted, you will find Switzerland, Singapore and all the Nordic countries there, i.e. small countries or city states. The co-founder of the index, Professor Paul Evans, does not consider this a coincidence in the interview printed between Chapters

Three and Four in this book. At his institute at INSEAD, they are presently looking into whether they should make a region/city index of talent attraction and development, rather than the keeping the present one, which works on national level.

Why is this happening? Why are regions and cities replacing nations as the key locus for talent attracting? Paul Evans sees a clear connection to the point of managing the ecosystem, the fifth element of the TAM model presented in Chapter Two. In order to face a challenge or do something about it, you both need to feel the same sense of urgency and work together with agility. This is easier at a regional/city level, where the number of stakeholders is smaller and the probability of developing a shared vision is bigger. Over the last few decades, we have seen several examples of remarkable change at the city/region level. Consider the perception we have now of Bilbao, Eindhoven and Manchester compared to a few years ago. That kind of significant change is more complex to conduct at the national level.

Two more reasons can be added to why cities and regions are the new locus for talent attraction. First, changes in financial possibilities on a national level matters. Many talent attraction initiatives have started through policies via financial means stemming from national government funds. Denmark serves as an example in this case. In 2006, the government launched the so-called 'Globalisation Strategy' to prepare Denmark for a more global world. One of the initiatives for talent attraction was the 'Fund for marketing Denmark internationally'. However, after the financial crisis at the end of the last decade, the fund was closed down. Today, it is not high on the national political agenda to spend money on talent attraction. Instead, the regions and cities themselves have to invest and conduct the necessary activities.

The second reason is that the brand of a city or a region is more unique and less complex than that of a country. Ireland and Dublin is a good example. For many years, the country 'Ireland' itself has been at the forefront in attracting companies and highly skilled people. 'ConnectIreland' or 'Invest in Ireland' (IDA Ireland) were two campaigns historically used for attracting international companies and talent. However, in talent attraction contexts today, you are more likely to see the name of 'Dublin' instead of Ireland: 'Become a Dubliner' or 'Dublin – a breath of fresh air'. Even though Ireland is not a huge country, it is still very varied, from a rugged west coast and green pastures to a thriving capital. Brand-wise, such a range of offerings makes telling your story more complex. Dublin is a more unique brand; it is easier to tell the story of what you will get if you move to Dublin. Likewise, the complexity of the stakeholder framework in the capital region is smaller, making it easier for them to establish specific soft-landing procedures and so on.

Finally, the new role of cities – the so-called 'urban age' – plays a role here too. As a global megatrend, some cities are becoming prominent international actors in their own right, often bypassing national governments. Add to that the ongoing urbanisation of economic activity, concentrating many jobs in growing urban regions, this further enhances the importance of cities in talent attraction.

Use the assets you have. Copenhagen will never be New York, Shanghai or Paris but it might be the first carbon neutral metropolis in the world. That is a real asset. Young professionals want to live in places with growth and interesting career opportunities, but even more so, if they can have these things in a sustainable location. Likewise (and this is something that should not be underestimated), clean air and short commuting times are both assets smaller metropolises around the world can use.

Are we ready for true brain circulation?

Europe is currently experiencing a strong political trend driven by populism, extreme right-wing influences, protectionism and, in some cases, even increased xenophobia. For example, a traditionally open country such as the UK has, in the last few years, taken steps to restrict access to their labour market for e.g. international students and, following the Brexit vote, possibly also other Europeans.

No doubt, meeting this challenge will require a strong political stance, unity from traditional political parties and efforts in communicating to the public the necessity of a new view on immigrant skills and talent mobility. Talent attraction efforts will be a waste of money in a country that at the same time permits political populism and xenophobia to set the agenda on immigration.

It will also take active efforts to develop a 'cultural intelligence' among those working in our public sector organisations, universities and companies in order to make them welcoming hosts and colleagues to any newcomers joining these organisations.

The new black: Management style and lifestyle as attraction factors

In the past, it has been the general opinion that talent moves primarily for the job. Research has indicated that the reason a person relocates to another place is an interesting job somewhere else, and when the job is there and they have got that in place, they then start looking at the place.[23] Young professionals with a preference for career-boosting jobs focus more on the content of the job: is it interesting, will it allow me to work with the things that are close to my heart, and can I develop my skills further?

Now, we are seeing that lifestyle factors as well as management style are becoming increasingly important in the choices of talented people. Urban theorist Richard Florida and others have published a variety of research on the topic of relocation. People like Manas Mani, interviewed earlier in this book, may have originally moved for the job and study opportunities, but the place and its lifestyle as well as management style and work culture mattered in their choice. Two other recent examples include:

1) Professor Charlie Marcus – what on earth made a world-leading professor in physics at Harvard University leave his job and transfer to a position as professor at University of Copenhagen, relocating his family of four? Of course, a lot of effort was put in by Copenhagen University in order to secure the right funding and framework for the research he is conducting, but lifestyle factors were important as well. The fact that his kids could move around by themselves in a safe and clean environment mattered in the decision-making process. Similarly, the work culture at the university, with a high degree of responsibility delegated to all team members including master students and PhDs, helped influence his final decision.

2) Young professionals relocating from London to Copenhagen – why move from a world leading metropolis to the capital of an odd country up north? Recently, a young, well-educated British couple made it into the national news in Denmark, mainly because of the reasons for their move.

---

23 Oxford Research (2014) and Niedomysl & Hansen (2010)

Essentially, they were looking for a different lifestyle. They were fed up with spending many hours every day getting from home to work. They thought the tempo of both private and professional life in London had reached a level where they were beginning to be concerned about the long-term health consequences. Finally, they could not see themselves building a family there. These lifestyle factors made Copenhagen an attractive alternative.

Lifestyle factors might not be a new consideration, but the tendency that people now go to the cool places and then find out what they can do there is new. Hot spots like Toronto and Berlin are good cases here. Just the global awareness that there is a vibrant and international environment in these places makes them attractive. That is also why attracting entrepreneurs is important. They add another flavour to a place with their different approaches to working and living. And as we discuss in Chapter Two, lifestyle factors may differ in importance between different target groups.

Besides lifestyle factors, management culture can be an asset in talent attraction as well. As mentioned by Paul Evans in the interview, the north European management style of trusting people, encouraging them to speak up and have an opinion or giving recent graduates responsibility at a relatively young age might be a hidden asset that could be further exploited in talent attraction. He considers the new generation – the Millennials – as being driven by opportunities and passion, explaining why they will be attracted to places where they are trusted and can grow as professionals and individuals. Seen from this perspective, some management styles will be considered more attractive than others. For example, the north European management style is often seen as an advantage compared to more hierarchical management styles elsewhere.

Is innovation in talent attraction still needed?

Perhaps the question should be rephrased: Has every idea been exhausted? Is it possible to keep finding new methods to stand out in the race for attracting the talent you need? And is 'innovation' just a buzzword that within a short time will be replaced with another new trend?

The answers vary. Let us take each question one by one. Have we exhausted all the ideas? Of course not – something new can always be developed. Your location has something unique to offer, you 'just' need to identify it, refine it to make it a value proposition for international talents and then find a method to get the message across to the world.

Use the TAM model as a framework for working with your local stakeholders. What is it that your city or region has to offer? Is it the jobs that give unique career possibilities? Is it the lifestyle that makes your region something special? Or can you put a soft-landing package together that ensures expat families will always talk positively about you? The options are numerous and it might not just be one factor that makes you stand out. It might be a combination of several things. Therefore, you need to spend some time developing your value proposition. This is not an easy endeavour, nor should you expect a quick turnaround. Nevertheless, the time and money invested is well spent. Benchmark a lot, dive more into the cases presented in this book and/or investigate some other destinations that are similar to your own. If you go to market too early, your message might not be specific enough or properly backed by your local partners. This could lead to disappointments among the talents you attract or among your local partners – you do not want either.

Try something new to stand out in today's world of communication overload. If your story does not get across to the talents you are looking for, try something new and try again. The more unknown you are or the more you need to change a certain existing perception of your location, the more innovative you have to be. You do not necessarily have to make the most noise or buy advertisements – remember, action speaks louder than words. Take the example of Jönköping in Sweden: plenty of research, some carefully targeted adverts and a free web shop for relocating talent. They did not have to buy media. Earned media is the goal: their social media activity spilled over into the press automatically. Or consider the 'ConnectIreland' initiative. The campaign created buzz by actually giving out rewards to people with tips that lead to new companies setting up new businesses in Ireland. Again, such activities stand out and will get your message across, not only to the media but eventually to the talent you would like to attract.

To address the second question, is it possible to keep finding new methods to attract talent? Of course it i,s and you simply need to keep reinventing your approach to the work, the value propositions you develop and the services you offer. Our suggestion is to further exploit the methods in innovation theory. Co-creation and user-driven innovation are well-proven concepts within innovation theory. They could be practised much more in talent attraction because no-one knows better what attracts and retains them than the international talents themselves. Involve them from the very beginning, maybe starting with talent you have already attracted. Why have they chosen your destination, what made them move and what are their suggestions for your next move? Likewise, you can reach out to the next ones to arrive. Be innovative in your approach here as well. Ask them to come up with their worst prejudice about your location and reward the winner with a myth-killer trip to come visit you. Ask them to upload videos with encounters with people from your locations and invite the most promising talent together with the person in the video to a restaurant and job site visit. The material and insights from such initiatives can be very useful.

The more you can get the people you want to attract involved in telling the story about your location and actually developing solutions, the better. If you were to relocate to a new location in another country, who would you trust the most: a marketing professional paid to tell a story or a former colleague from your own country who already has made the journey with success? You know the answer. But it is more than the story, it is also the ideas and solutions about how to improve your location's value proposition. The international talent already working and living in your place encounter difficulties on an everyday basis, and since they are bright-minded individuals, they cannot help thinking of possible solutions. Tapping into that pool of knowledge can potentially be your biggest asset. In addition to the innovative approach, you also have to be much more targeted. Drawing on some good old marketing and sales methods: if you do not know your customer, you will not know how to reach them either.

A final question to consider is whether the word 'innovation' in innovating talent attraction may be replaced by some other buzzword yet to be coined. The reason why our answer is 'maybe' and not just 'that is surely what is going to happen' is that the need for innovation is immense. As we have stated several times throughout this book, you have to be smart, come up with new ideas and be able to implement them together with your local stakeholders in order to be attractive for international talent. Those are great virtues in innovation theory and in our opinion should be exploited much more than at present. This is the reason why we insist on saying that innovating talent attraction might be replaced by a new trend and buzzword within a not-too-distant future – because eventually it will. Those working within talent attraction are talented and entrepreneurial people themselves and they will keep on developing new methods and frameworks for their work. That is why it is so much fun to be working within the field of talent attraction. Reinventing yourself and developing your region and city is vital for success. If not, others will be better at attracting the people you need. But we are true believers; if we are all passionate about improving our surroundings, we collectively make the world a better place to live. Have you ever thought of relocating to another country?

References

European Union Regional Policy (2008). *Labour mobility between the regions of the EU-27 and a comparison with the USA,* Regional Focus. http://ec.europa.eu/regional_policy/sources/docgener/focus/2008_02_labour.pdf. September 23, 2016.

Izquierdo, M., Jimeno, J.F., & Lacuesta, A. (2015). *Spain: From immigration to emigration*. Banco de Espana.

Niedomysl, T. & Hansen, H.K. (2010). What matters more for the decision to move: jobs versus amenities. *Environment and Planning A* 42(7).

Oxford Research (2014). *Expat Study 2014*. http://www.copcap.com/news-list/2014/expat-study-2014-denmark-is-great-for-career-and-family-life. September 23, 2016.

About the authors

Marcus Andersson currently serves as the Head of Unit for Migration Intelligence at the Swedish Migration Agency, providing the executive management and the Swedish government with actionable intelligence on international migration flows. He is also Chairman, Co-founder and former CEO of Tendensor International, an international strategy consultancy focusing on place attractiveness, as well as Co-founder of Nordic Place Academy. Previously, he has worked for the Swedish Ministry of Enterprise and Innovation and the European Commission in policy areas such as innovation, cluster development and entrepreneurship. He is also a trained intelligence analyst and has worked as an intelligence officer for the Swedish Security Service. Being a keen writer, he has published a range of academic papers, articles and handbooks on topics such as talent attraction, investment promotion, cluster development and place branding.

Morten King-Grubert has been everything from an intern to a managing director based out of Denmark, the United Kingdom, Austria and the U.S. Having launched his career within the Trade Council of the Danish Ministry of Foreign Affairs helping Danish companies export goods and services internationally, he has subsequently spent seven years as one of the main architects behind Copenhagen Capacity's talent attraction and retention efforts. In recent years, Morten has advised cities, regions and countries all over Europe on how to reach their target group within talent attraction and retention. Currently, Morten is directing the market entry of the leading fintech company Creamfinance into Denmark, and serving as a professor and career counsellor to international talents at DIS Copenhagen. He is also the author of the book *The Mermaid Dialogue*.

Nikolaj Lubanski is Director for Talent Attraction at Copenhagen Capacity, the official investment promotion agency of Greater Copenhagen. Nikolaj has served both as CEO and Manager for a number of private and public institutes, driven by a passion to improve the society we live in through globalisation. He is passionate about research and knowledge-sharing, and is the author of several books and publications within the area of innovation, labour-market issues and management. He likes to share and develop his thoughts through participation as a speaker and panellist at international conferences. Born to a Polish-Danish family and having worked in several countries, international mobility lies at the heart of everything he does.

Acknowledgements

This project could not have been completed without help from many business partners and collaborators located all over the world. A warm and heartfelt thank you from all three of us to:

- Copenhagen Capacity, Tendensor and Nordic Place Academy for providing first-class resources, knowledge and data;
- our lead researcher Katarzyna Dygul and contributing editor Alexa Newlin, whose contributions are evident throughout the entire book;
- Dagmar Irgang, research assistant at Copenhagen Capacity, for sharing a helping hand in times of need;
- the wonderful individuals who volunteered to be interviewed for this book and provided highly relevant content and considerations for the context of our practitioner's guide: Charlotte Mark, His Royal Highness Prince Joachim, Manas Mani, Merlind Hinz, Paul Evans and Yvonne van Hest;
- the multiple organisations who shared their business insights with us, making the cases and regional examples available to our readers, including among others: Berlin Partner, Start Up Chile, Tampere Region Economic Development Agency, Business Oulu, Copenhagen Capacity, Brainport Development, Tel Aviv Global, Start Up Nation Central, Dual Citizen LLC, Sustainability and Economic Development Collaboratory (SEDC), Singapore, Nanyang Technological University, Singapore, Ontario Ministry of Research and Innovation, Scottish Enterprise, Bizkaia:talent, Montréal International, CityStudio Vancouver, Destination Jönköping, Demola, Vaasa Region Development Company, Marketing Manchester, Stockholm Business Region and Global Talent Gothenburg/West Sweden; and
- our publisher Mads Julius Elf and the wonderful team at U Press for believing in the original idea and providing excellent feedback throughout the project.

Finally, this book was written in a fantastic spirit of teamwork and equal contribution among ourselves as authors. Our personal thank yous are extended to our families for their continuous support for our endeavours, as crazy as they may be sometimes. Thank you Shelby and Axel King-Grubert; Carina, Edith and Harry Fornegård-Andersson; and Maria, Asta, Olga, Solveig and Zakarias Lubanski.

Appendix overview

Appendix 1 – Regional assessment survey

Appendix 2 – Cases
- Case 1: Austin mini case – Attracting talent by supporting creativity
- Case 2: Berlin mini case – The role of the public sector in an organically developed ecosystem
- Case 3: Bizkaia mini case – A network-model approach to talent attraction
- Case 4: Chile mini case – Building a brand by going against the grain
- Case 5: Brainport mini case – From the 'war for talent' to talent sharing
- Case 6: Singapore mini case – A key pillar in the country's economic strategy
- Case 7: Tampere mini case – Providing local help to talents
- Case 8: Tel Aviv mini case – Entrepreneurial culture
- Case 9: Toronto mini case – Immigration policy as a talent magnet

Appendix 1 – Regional assessment survey

It is our sincere hope that this book's usefulness does not end with its final chapter. Instead, we intend for it to serve as a practitioner's guide to individuals acting on behalf of cities, regions and countries seeking to develop both their strategy and operational activities to attract and retain international talent.

And now, we pass the torch to you.

We have explained that in a world with fierce competition to achieve the attention of bright minds, you need to do something extraordinary. You need an innovative approach to talent attraction. By gathering the newest knowledge and best-case examples from different locations across Europe and the world, this book can serve as your guide. But it is you who must act.

To help you get started, we have developed a regional assessments survey that we have successfully used in our work with selected talent attraction entities around the world.

Ideally, we would like you to sit down with your colleagues and key stakeholders and complete this exercise together, but feel free to start it on your own if that is more practical.

The departure point for the survey is our Talent Attraction Management model and the five key cornerstones of talent attraction – talent reception, talent integration, talent reputation and management of the ecosystem.

For each of the five focus areas of our model, we first ask you to score how important each area is to your region based on a scale of 1 to 10 (1 being not important and 10 very important). Perhaps you are like Berlin and international entrepreneurs are coming to your region en masse, so attraction is not that important? In this case, perhaps you might rate this area a 2.

Following this overall assessment, we have four to five key questions in each subcategory allowing you to identify where specific improvements could be made. Again use a score of 1 to 10 as you rank yourself – 'yourself' being not just your organisation, but activities in your region as a whole.

Remember, be as honest as possible about your accomplishments, as the purpose of this exercise is not to make you look good. Once you have completed the survey we encourage you to review your score and use it to prioritise an area of improvement. First, compare how you score overall on the five main focus areas. Do you have one or two substantially low scores? Then this is probably where you should start. Secondly, review all the questions to identify specific areas where you could optimise the value you create.

Now it is time to brainstorm. What can you actually do to improve your efforts? Hopefully by now you will have considered many of the case examples from this book and be able to innovate on top of these concepts. Then you are well equipped to outline your action plan in more detail.

We wish you the best of luck.

Regional Assessment Survey

Focus area	Score
How important is **talent attraction** to your region?	
Are you targeted in your marketing approach?	
Are employers close partners in your talent attraction activities?	
Can you attract followers on your social media platforms?	
Are your target groups of talents engaged in your activities (e.g. are there opportunities for them to "click" on what you want them to, sign up to a database, apply for a job etc.)?	
How important is **talent reception** to your region?	
Is it clear to international talents where to find general information about the region related to relocation?	
Does your region have a digital (or print) relocation guide outlining what the relocating talent needs to do before and after arrival?	
Have you adopted a one-stop shop process, where the international talent can get every administrative detail covered in one go (a digital or physical "International House"?)	
How important is talent integration to your region?	
How would you rank the level and quality of social activities?	
How would you rank the level and quality of professional activities?	
To what extent are international students retained after graduation?	
Do senior professionals stay "long enough" in your region?	
How important is talent reputation to your region?	
Do you have place branding material that companies like and use?	
Are you engaging ambassadors to tell your story?	
Do you have an overall branding strategy for your location?	
How important is management of the ecosystem to your region?	
Do you have a regional TAM strategy involving multiple organisations?	
Are the activities and stakeholder commitments sustainable over time?	
Has a system/governance been put in place to coordinate and facilitate activities carried out by an ecosystem of different organisations?	
Do your stakeholders (employers, politicians, universities etc.) believe in attracting international talent?	
Can you measure the economic impact of your activities?	

Appendix 2 – Cases

These case studies stem from different benchmarking, development and research projects carried out by Tendensor, Tendensor International and Nordic Place Academy between 2013 and 2016. The main purpose of the case studies is to generate inspirational advice and ideas for other locations to follow when implementing their own strategies and activities.

All the cases can be accessed at www.tendensor.com/TAMcases.

Case 1:   Austin mini case – Attracting talent by supporting creativity

A lack of strong traditional industries in the local economy can allow space for innovative place branding approaches. Culture and creativity might just be the best selling point one could ask for.

Many regard Austin (picture p. 72/73) as one of the world's hotspots for creative talent and innovation. This can be largely attributed to the city's effective mixture of deliberate strategies and less tangible but equally impactful initiatives positively influencing talent attraction in Austin.

One of the predominant and concrete initiatives behind Austin's success is the internationally acclaimed **South By Southwest Festival** (SXSW). Over 29 years of SXSW's history, Austin managed to leverage the festival's talent attraction potential to continuously improve the city's appeal and infrastructure needed for talent attraction, retention and development.

SXSW combines creative arts and emerging technologies into a festival concept; it is not only a talent magnet itself, but it also contributes to the city's branding strategy at large. Austin and SXSW can be seen as a melting pot for creatives, established tech professionals and entrepreneurs, entering through the festival "portal" and forging connections with local and external talents.

Another strategic move that paved Austin's road to success is the focused and disciplined cooperation between public and private actors.

In the early 2000s, Austin experienced an economic downturn, which brought a need for a coordinated action plan to revise the city's talent attraction activities. Public and private actors developed a number of activities that have successfully boosted job creation, graduation rate, inflow of talent and corporate relocation. The flagship initiative of this cooperation, **Opportunity Austin**, prioritises talent development and attraction as well as creating conditions for start-ups and businesses to thrive. The city's dedication to valuing and nurturing creativity and commerce built an image of a strong creative scene with career-building opportunities.

Consequently, the strong image of the region seems to be corresponding to the identity of Austin, which despite being a rather intangible factor, has contributed largely to Austin's position as a creative, inclusive and technology-driven city. The importance of being "authentic" and staying original is also emphasised, and the SXSW can be seen as a clear expression of Austin's authenticity and its creative cachet.

Key learning points:

- The direct impact on talent attraction and retention of the SXSW festival is difficult to estimate for obvious reasons; however, given the years of significant impact on Austin's creative economy and the vast media coverage, the reputation of a creative, forward-thinking place is beyond doubt.
- Public–private complementary activities and dedication to nurturing creativity and commerce builds a brand appreciated by both talents and companies.
- Authenticity and culture can be used as a stronghold of the location, introducing the spirit of a place to outsiders and nurturing identity internally.

Case 2: Berlin mini case – The role of the public sector in an organically developed ecosystem

When considering what role the public sector can play in a well-functioning, organically developed ecosystem, look no further than Berlin (picture p. 24/25). As one of the fastest growing start-up ecosystems in the world, Berlin is the European flagship within talent attraction. Due to the city's best selling points – diversity, low living costs and a rich cultural life – it became a magnet for creatives and techies alike and is often described as the place where "punk meets tech", an appealing brand for young talent and entrepreneurs.

The natural inflow of talent, particularly in the creative field and IT, led to an organic and market-driven start-up ecosystem development, which grew without much support from the public sector in its first years. Entrepreneurs engaged in creating co-working spaces and start-up events gradually generated a bustling start-up scene. Big IPOs as well as international publicity linked to famous investors in the Berlin start-ups created a knock-on effect, where the region gained a reputation for being cool, resulting in exponential growth in the aftermath of these success stories.

From the public sector perspective, facilitating talent management was originally posed as a challenge as the system seemed to function without support. Consequently, the focus predominantly targeted the talent already attracted to the city. However, identifying market failures and developing measures is where the public sector could really add value. This approach manifested in a number of public and public–private initiatives. To start with, these initiatives provided the ground for talent retention, development and management activities, particularly connected to optimising business immigration services (work permits). By limiting red tape in all public touch points for start-ups, it allowed opportunities to make financing available through public rounds and develop existing talent through supporting these growth areas.

An inspiring initiative, directly linked to the successes of the work permit optimisation, is the collaboration between Berlin and Silicon Valley. Here, the start-ups' founders are invited to relocate to Berlin to help scale or support the IPO of local start-ups.

Another great example is Berlin's international cooperation on talent sharing, with a pilot programme set up between New York and Tel Aviv.

In summary, the ecosystem is benefiting immensely from the public sector support strategy – today becoming almost self-sustainable and growing through brand and perception value.

Key learning points:

- Understand what drives your ecosystem and work strategically to address market failures, to position yourself successfully in supporting talent and entrepreneurs.
- Utilise existing attraction factors, such as the creative spirit of your region. This can function as a catalyst for talent attraction.
- Consider how you can position yourself with regards to international partners and ecosystems. Identify your "Silicon Valley" peer-to-peer collaborator and work on your value proposition.
- Find your unique selling points. Inexpensive living costs and an open-minded, diversified community can act as a magnet for international and local talent.

Case 3:   Bizkaia mini case – A network-model approach to talent attraction

Many countries and communities that have experienced brain drain in the last decade are searching for inspiration on how to re-attract their expatriated talent and prepare for future demographic challenges. The Basque Country (Bizkaia picture p. 8/9) serves as an interesting example, particularly since it is a small region of 1.2 million inhabitants with a strong cultural identity – an identity which is smartly being implemented in place branding and talent attraction. With its neighbouring metropolitan competitors such as Madrid and Barcelona, the Basque Country aims at positioning itself on the talent map through network building as well as working with talent mobility on a European scale.

Bizkaia:talent, the organisation responsible for talent attraction management, applies a long-term approach in its efforts, with one of its most inspiring activities centred around provision of service to top university students via the Talentia Service programme and attraction of highly qualified talent through the Be Basque Talent Network.

The Be Basque Talent Network builds on a strong feeling of cultural identity and provides an online networking platform for talent and companies that are Basque at heart – meaning those who have been, are or want to be related to the region, regardless of their territorial origin. Here, talent should be understood as highly qualified professionals, with at least one university degree. The network provides its users with access to a specific profile, job openings, information exchange forum and discussion about work-related issues in the Basque Country. The service has a talent search map, allowing interested parties to find different members by residence, origin, sector/industry and what type of job may interest them.

The Talentia Service works with domestic students to upgrade top graduates from 'academics' to actual labour force candidates and match them for company competence needs through career counselling, company visits and networking opportunities.

With limited local human capital resources and a need to build the brand of the region, Bizkaia:talent believes in fostering talent circulation and is therefore a founding member of the European Regional Talent Mobility Network (EuRetalent). The exchange of innovative practices on talent mobility management between European regions and international partners is at the core of this initiative, with the overarching goal of increasing regional innovation and competitiveness.

Case 4: Chile mini case – Building a brand by going against the grain

Many countries and cities globally are beginning to harness the entrepreneurial spirit already present in their communities. But what if your city or region just does not have any? Chile has the answer (Santiago picture p. 126/127).

In the past, Chile was far from being associated with a rich talent pool or strong entrepreneurial spirit. It all changed in 2010 when the Chilean government took an experimental approach and made a bet – investing in foreign entrepreneurs and creating the opportunity for them to interact with locals would lead to increased talent circulation. It not only worked, but in turn built a strong base of Chilean talent. Chile successfully applied a 'concept-based talent attraction management strategy' for places by developing a 'unique place offering' to international entrepreneurs and start-ups. This approach can be replicated by any city or region.

Since its launch in 2010, the Start-Up Chile (SUP) programme has attracted almost 20,000 applicants from more than 120 countries, with a

30 percent participation rate of Chilean citizens. Today, SUP can showcase results on the local economy and culture, which in the case of Chile is of equal importance. The biggest ambition for SUP is to change the local risk-averse mind-set and spur local entrepreneurship.

The main attraction factors behind SUP form an approach called "live, work, play", which includes: providing equity-free seed capital of $40,000 USD, a one-year visa, soft-landing services for the entrepreneur and access to the Latin America Market and its networking opportunities.

For obvious reasons, the strategy of "giving out" money to foreign entrepreneurs was an uncommon approach. However, its disruptiveness resonated with the target audience (the entrepreneurs), and paired with a fast-track immigration process, earned Chile a strong position in the global start-up community. One of the unique benefits of participating in the programme is that all programme participants are exposed to a real cultural experience and a history-making opportunity. This acts as a self-reinforcing effect, since all programme participants are enrolled in the SUP alumni network upon graduation, allowing for co-created marketing. The alumni not only promote SUP in their home environments but also collaborate with local embassies around the world in order to facilitate free meet-ups and workshops.

Continuing to evolve, spin-offs from the core programme have emerged, utilising the already existing organisational resources and targeting special types of talents. Examples include targeting female entrepreneurs through the S-Factory or targeting scaling up challenges through the Scale Up initiative.

Key learning points:

- Start-up Chile has created value by going against the grain. Searching for disruptive approaches can help build the brand of your region.
- By taking a community-based approach and engaging programme participants, co-creation and co-marketing can be enabled.
- Accentuate your strengths, and do so in an authentic and disruptive manner.
- Ensuring a soft landing can help attract and integrate talents and spouses alike.

- Empowering entrepreneurs and connecting them with critical resources is a powerful way to foster investment, economic growth and innovation.

Case 5:   Brainport mini case – From the war for talent to talent sharing

Talent mobility is an increasing global trend, which can be considered as both a challenge and an opportunity. Brainport (Eindhoven picture p. 112/113) is an insightful example of how to explore the opportunity via its strategy of utilising a market-driven approach to develop long-term public–private partnerships in talent attraction.

The Brainport Eindhoven region in the Netherlands has been working with talent attraction and retention since 2007, continuously reviewing and refreshing its activities. From a global labor market perspective, it has managed to build a strong brand in a relatively short time. Innovative and adept in international talent attraction and talent sharing programmes, Brainport deploys a number of activities that contribute to its success:

1. The public–private organisational model should be seen as a key enabler to talent attraction programmes and Brainport Development (Brainport's regional development agency) – as their key driver. The talent attraction and retention activities are 75 percent funded by the private sector, and are carried out through the public–private partnership comprising of Brainport Development and 28 additional companies and knowledge institutes.

2. The talent attraction funding strategy, following market demand, distinctively shaped Brainport's talent activities of today. Involving companies early in the process of talent attraction, combined with the idea to deliver 'proof of concept' to them, makes it possible to tailor services to the needs of the companies and thereby meet their demand for talent.

3. Their talent sharing portal – the TalentBOX – is an agile response to the current trend of talent shortage. It is an online portal for local and international tech and IT talents to find jobs, knowledge and networks. It functions as both a marketing and information portal, as well as a tool for recruitment and engagement with the targeted group of local and international talent, allowing them to share their peer-to-peer stories and experiences. One of its most interesting features is the semantic searches

and matching function, enabling both candidate and employer to see their respective matches. TalentBOX also enables employers to share and recommend the qualified talent that participated in their respective recruitment processes but did not lead to a hired position. This feature provides the applicant not only with a recommendation, but also with the prospect of future employment with a more suitable company.

Key learning points:

- Promote and facilitate talent mobility and talent sharing between employers, creating a more attractive ecosystem.
- Offer relevant professional content that can help local and international professionals find jobs and develop their careers in the region or elsewhere.
- To stay relevant, follow the market demand and work with stakeholders – and taking a cue from Brainport, always keep in mind your target audience and the purpose of your activities.

Case 6: Singapore mini case – A key pillar in the country's economic strategy

Long-term strategy is often the key to success, particularly with regards to positioning oneself on a global map for talent attraction. Singapore's (picture p. 40/41) relentless commitment to the matter gives great insight into how to build a world-class economy based on talent acquisition.

Singapore does not have any significant natural resources and available land is becoming increasingly scarce. This has forced it to take innovative and long-term measures to secure the economic success of the country. For nearly 60 years, talent attraction has played an important role and has helped Singapore secure a number of innovative businesses within cleantech, financial services, biomedical services and creative industries.

Despite private business constituting the majority of the economy, the public industry and the Singaporean government play an active role in nurturing the ground for the private sector by helping it secure the demand for talent and human capital. The Economic Development Board of the Singaporean Government plans and executes a number of strategies to sustain Singapore as a global leader. These include connecting different private and public communities, taking active steps to reduce red tape and initiating a number of branding campaigns. Education is another important pillar in Singapore's talent supply, with the strategy of making Singapore a "global schoolhouse" – both by strengthening education from the bottom up, and by attracting world-class universities to set up campuses in the country. This has ensured talent supply both through attracting foreign talent as well as educating local talent.

Key learning points:

- Balancing the relationship between private and public helps remove bottle-necks. In Singapore, this has been achieved through legitimisation and support of private efforts to secure talent supply.
- As land and natural resources become increasingly scarce, talent becomes the most important resource for securing long-term growth. Singapore has been affected by a lack of natural resources, which has forced the country to focus on talent attraction to support innovative businesses.
- Singapore has managed to become an intellectual hub by attracting world-class universities from around the world through its "brain strategy".

Case 7: Tampere mini case – Providing local help to talents

Talent attraction management might increasingly become a priority on the regional development agenda of many locations globally, however the fact is that smaller cities and regions still struggle to get institutional and financial support to establish adequate programmes and management structures pertaining to talent attraction. Tampere city (picture p. 144/145) in Finland exemplifies a place with a concept and persistency in talent-related activities, making it a relatable case for many.

Tampere is one of very few cities/regions in northern Europe where specific talent attraction-related positions have been created. This case is particularly interesting in the light of the fact that the Tampere region has 365,000 inhabitants, with 40,000 being students.

Additionally, although there is a certain surplus of Nokia IT staff after layoffs in recent years, Tampere still wants more talent and the general consensus in the region is that talent, ideally international, is needed to boost companies' creativity and innovation capacities.

That approach led to a strategy to bring a talent attraction and retention organisation to life.

The Tampere Region Economic Development Agency (Tradea) took the lead and formed a quadruple-helix collaboration model to address the matter and provide networks, mentoring and soft-landing services. The dedicated Talent Attraction Team is given the mandate to coordinate the various activities.

One such initiative is Talent Tampere, a network that develops tools for talent attraction and is open to all organisations/initiatives. The network is actually a collection of professional and social networks that connect locals, internationals, students, talents and companies, facilitating two-way exchanges for both job seekers and companies looking for international competences. It is noteworthy that one of the aims of and ways to work with this is to involve talents themselves in development and innovation environments. As a result, the expats are not seen only as subjects of economy or labour, but are as involved in the activities and local agenda as the stakeholders. This makes the city and region more attractive as an investment, working and living destination.

While Talent Tampere Network is currently financed by City of Tampere through its Economic Development Fund, other stakeholders contribute with their time, voluntary work or project sponsorships, thus giving Talent Tampere Network purpose and content.

Key learning points:

- Creating a dedicated talent attraction department and team enables initiatives that address not only the status quo but also improve general economic perspectives for the region.
- Focus local efforts to help talents with improving their networks, job-hunting skills and finding out about professional opportunities in the region.

- International students can work closely with local companies, giving them a chance to get to know the local business and work culture, which makes it more likely that they will stay and work in the location.

Case 8: Tel Aviv mini case – Entrepreneurial culture

Tel Aviv (picture p. 92/93), nicknamed the "Startup City", claims to occupy first place in the international ranking of start-up ecosystems outside of the US, with its striking number of start-ups equal to one for every 431 residents. Tel Aviv tells a great story of how to transform a small and isolated city into a frontrunner in technology and innovation with plenty of highly skilled and entrepreneurial talent.

Within the entrepreneurial talent management field, it is the culture and holistic approach in the general ecosystem of growth and development that sets Tel Aviv apart. The Israeli people cultivate a risk-taking approach, and the ability to fail successfully and start over is perceived positively within the ecosystem. The local market size poses natural constraints, and therefore local companies are encouraged to think big in their business strategies. The Israeli military service also plays an important role in entrepreneurship development and support. In this environment, young people are exposed to real-life challenges along with the latest ground-breaking technology, helping talent to strive to create innovative solutions for all.

While Tel Aviv enjoys a steady supply of local talent, it is often still necessary for start-up founders to venture out to ensure the company's growth –to Silicon Valley, for example. With the appropriate risk-taking cultural mind-set, many founders decide to leverage this need by launching their operations in some of the bigger markets such as the U.S., while preserving their HQ in Tel Aviv.

Institutional and infrastructural support is provided by both the public and the private sectors. The local government provides around 20 incubators with funding of up to 85 percent. Due to close ties with the U.S. and many entrepreneurs becoming angel investors, access to further funding is likely.

Key learning points:

- Matching grants to VC funds and direct grants to start-ups is needed to enable local start-ups to grow.
- Setting up second offices abroad to foster company growth can be a great opportunity for the entire ecosystem, where tapping into a new talent pool and expertise can lead to spill-over effects.
- A positive image of the entrepreneurial career choice and a foundation in business risk-taking is needed for any entrepreneurial ecosystem.
- An entrepreneurial spirit can be stimulated by exposing people to innovation along with the need for new solutions to real problems and societal challenges (e.g. military, security, geopolitics, healthcare).
- From the start, leverage domestic market constraints by supporting entrepreneurial culture and promoting global thinking in business strategies.

Case 9: Toronto mini case – Immigration policy as a talent magnet

The concentration of highly skilled talent and a favourable immigration policy has placed Toronto (picture p. 58/59) on the global map, making it an inspiring case for how to develop a public vision and strategy to support talent attraction and utilise the entrepreneurial capacity of local immigrants.

The region of Ontario receives almost 100,000 immigrants per year and the majority of these have a high level of skill or are the family members of a skilled immigrant. As it turns out, it is often the same risk-taking and entrepreneurial spirit that drives these immigrants to move to a new country and later start their own business in Toronto. This is to some extent reflected in that fact that approximately 98 percent of all businesses in Toronto are small (under 100 employees). The city understands the value and contributions the entrepreneurial and small business culture has on the local economy. Therefore a strategy that utilises this kind of ethic and skill-set diversity is positioned high on the public agenda.

In particular, the Toronto Region Immigrant Employment Council (TRIEC) plays a role in attracting and supporting highly skilled immigrants.

It is a multi-stakeholder council that brings leadership together to create and champion solutions to better integrate skilled immigrants in the Toronto region labour market.[24] Through specifically designed programmes and networks, TRIEC is taking action on the under-utilisation of skilled immigrants' education, talent and experience.

Secondly, the Mayor of Toronto not only publicly supports this initiative but also assembles working groups comprising all major local stakeholders to figure out what the city can do to help entrepreneurs grow and thrive. The working group alone acts as a testament to the public support in the area, strengthening the positive image of entrepreneurship.

Furthermore, the geographical proximity to tech hubs such as Waterloo is leveraged by Toronto in creating a larger ecosystem, and expanding business opportunities for local and foreign talent interested in relocating. This can also be linked to the recent trend of native Toronto founders returning from Silicon Valley for lifestyle reasons, bringing angel and VC potential along, which ultimately contributes as an attraction factor for Toronto.

Key learning points:

- An open-minded immigration policy can boost your location's innovation capacity as well as its economic growth.
- Recognise the existing skills in your region and the economic value created from start-ups and small businesses. Support from the Mayor and/or other authoritative figures is a positive signal, contributing to the attractiveness of the place.
- Build a larger metropolis and ecosystem by connecting with strong regional partners, creating overall better business opportunities for talent.

---

24 Including employers, regulatory bodies, professional associations, educators, labour, community groups, government and immigrants.